AF581317

R E D H E A D S

R E D H E A D S

Photographs by Uwe Ditz

Texts by Uwe Ditz, Barry Egan and Irmela Hannover

EDITION STEMMLE

Zurich New York

I would like to thank all my models, the most of whom decided spontaneously to pose for the camera. Their trust made this work possible.

Contents

Redheads

Barry Egan

Blame Judas.

And not just for betraying Jesus Christ to the Romans either. If Judas Iscariot had had blonde hair instead of red, then perhaps our social history would have looked different. Then, for centuries, blondes would have been looked upon as being wicked, untrustworthy, emotionally dysfunctional deviants instead of us redheads. There has always been a sense that there's something odd—not quite normal—about people with red hair. We are made to feel ashamed about our freckles, our ugly white skin, our vile bodies.

There are innumerable stories—most of them negative—about the redheads and the supposed wrongdoings by us redheads. We were not to be trusted. Because of this untrustworthiness embedded in our nature, bees always sting redheads. Blondes are fickle and make false friends, brunettes are sincere and in good health while redheads are unstable and have terrible tempers. Sounds familiar?

In the Middle Ages, redheads were feared as the most potent of witches and sorcerers. They were also burnt at the stake. (Seth, the sorcerer brother of Osiris, was said to have been a redhead.) Since red is the color of fire, the Romans and Greeks thought they were unlucky people to have around. They also did unspeakable things to redheads. Red hot pokers up, well ... you don't want to know. In 15th century England, the fat of a dead red-haired person was much in demand as an ingredient for poison. Indeed, there is an old English saying that goes: "flattery, like the plague, strikes into the brain of man, and rageth in his entrails when he can, worse than the poison of a redhair'd man." It is thought that the feelings against red originated in England, because of the red-haired Vikings, who once invaded the country raping and killing and generally up to no good. While in Europe, the anti-redhead prejudice is ascribed to the fact that the aforesaid Judas Iscariot had such hair. But there's more to it than that. Let us go deeper. Let us not forget the Scarlet Letter—the red "A" worn by women convicted of adultery in the Puritan communities of New England. The term "Scarlet Woman" also means a "woman of loose morals, a whore." "Scarlet Woman" was also used by Protestant sects to describe what they saw as the wholly negative nature of the Catholic Church (and, in particular, Revelation 17). Satan, of course, isn't just the Antichrist. He is the red devil: trust the most famous manifestation of evil to also be a redhead.

In October 1916, the *Literary Digest* ran an intriguing and somewhat racist piece entitled "Chestnut Threads Among with Gold." Terrified that the white America was being swamped by alien skin colors, the author states that blondes, redheads and light brunettes are disappearing, because of the influx of Russian and Latin immigrants. In a moral panic, the author finally declares that all American hair will soon have a mud color: "Still, there is cheer; here and there the glorious redhaired girl still holds the fort, a brilliant spot of beauty in the wide monotony of brunettes?" Of course, many positive aspects of redheads have been pointed out as well. According to the Irish poet Yeats, "Red is the color of magic in every country and has been so from the very earliest times." Red is equated with emotion. It is also the color of passion. That's all well and good, but a negative connotation has stuck like glue to the word "red" to us. Being caught "red-handed" is to be caught in the middle of a crime while a "red herring" is to introduce an idea that will deliberately mislead someone away from the truth. To "paint the town red" is to go on a mad drinking binge. A "redneck" is a dirt-poor white American who lynched blacks in the Deep South. A "red shirt" is an revolutionary anarchist. And where do prostitutes congregate? In the "red-light district."

"Ginger nuts" and "Redser" were my nicknames at school. While it was largely a happy time, I once had my testicles ruptured after a bunch of guys repeatedly kicked me in the "red balls." "Kick Redser!" were the words I remembered afterwards at the doctor's, as I received stitches in my testicles. "I've tried to overcome being bitter about school," *Simply Red* singer Mick Hucknall wrote last year in *The Sunday Times,* "because there comes a point that unless you forget and forgive, it scars you for the rest of your life. I think I've gotten over it. I just pray that it's not happening to other redheads, or anybody who looks different in their school. I hope that teachers know how to better deal with what is fundamentally a very desperate time. But I look at people with red hair and I think: 'I'll guarantee you're having a hard time.' Any redhead will tell you that, at some point, they've had a bit of a rough ride, because they look different."

Ginger Spice was routinely referred to as the "Ugly Spice"—the Spice Girl nobody wanted to go to bed with. When she had a brief romantic interlude with fellow redhead, British TV presenter Chris Evans, the bile in the media was unprecedented. "Imagine what their children would look like," sneered one of the tabloids. I won't make too much of this much-vaunted anti-redhead prejudice in modern society into a theory of racism. We haven't been murdered because of our color, like so many thousand blacks in America were in the forties and the fifties. No. We were only ridiculed and made to feel unwanted because of our hair color. But there is a more viable theory that the strong character ascribed to redheads has been molded by prolonged exposure to negative press (if nothing else, it provided a productive environment for communal self-analysis.) Still, the social conditioning against redheads down through the centuries—however subtle—has had its effects. In response to a recent US magazine survey among 1,000 men on whether "gentlemen preferred blondes" redheads came in last—blondes were first ... This is hardly surprising. I mean, name me one Hollywood star with red hair? Apart from Nicole Kidman? You can't, can you? Ditto the fashion world. Although pale complexions are returning to fashion the fashion editors/photographers/designers are responsible for contributing to the warped aesthetic. There are no supermodels with red hair. Perhaps the title of Naomi Wolf's next book should be *The Beauty Myth: Why Redheads Are Gorgeous Too.*

There has been an undoubted and radical shift in our consciousness over the last few years. We have taken on the mantra of the black civil rights activists during the sixties in America: "Say It Loud, We're Red and We're Proud." I realize now what I never understood before: being a redhead today is a magnificent thing. We stand out. Not like a sore thumb. We stand out like a beautiful Renaissance painting in a room full of yellowing Pamela Anderson posters. We're one *in* a million—not one of the millions of those tall, dark and handsome people out there. We've stopped worrying and learnt to love ourselves. That doesn't mean that modern society is loving us yet, though. I believe that red-haired people are still generally considered to be unattractive. We are considered outside the norm. We are a genetic curiosity, an intriguing anatomical creation. Certainly, for a long time being a redhead was a life of moral deformity, spiritual impoverishment and everyday humiliation.

We learnt to hate our bodies—to despise that red face that looked back at us in the mirror every morning. You got laughed at in the showers in school after rugby practice. At least I did. You were disgusted by your own body. At least I was. You hated those little red curls down there and the pain they brought into your life. You dreamt of having black hair—and of being tall, dark and handsome as opposed to small, red and loathsome. I hated my hair. I hated my freckles. I hated myself. I wanted to be Elvis Presley. I wanted black hair. Having red hair felt like a life-long curse that couldn't be lifted. And it seemed like red pubic hair was the ultimate physical deformity. Girls would make jokes about boys with "ginger pubes." The big fear about losing my virginity was not that I wouldn't be able to perform—that was taken for granted—but rather that the poor girl in question would run out of the room in horror when she saw the color of my pubic hair. Perhaps it should have dawned on me that she might have had some earlier indication from the hair on my head. But then life is never so clear when you're 28—sorry, I mean 17. In any event, I felt like Woody Allen trapped in a red unwanted body. I thought there couldn't possibly be a girl out there who'd want to have sex with a red head. Not even a redhead girl.

It took me ten years to realize just how wonderful having red hair is. (Let women think that you had the fiery temperament they all wanted: in any event, the temper-myth probably added to your sexual mystique). You realized that women liked you precisely for the same reason they used to laugh at you when you were a kid: because you are different. The color of your hair gave you a certain character, an aura of the decidedly extraordinary. It was a moment of clarity—a defining moment when it all made sense. Suddenly, I was beautiful.
And my red pubic hair most of all ...

Women with Red Hair

Irmela Hannover

When I was born 45 years ago, we had already survived the worst. No one accused my mother of having courted the devil because she had given birth to a redheaded daughter, although she herself was a brunette. There were also no suggestions that she had fallen victim to the evil eye whilst pregnant, nor that she had stared into the oven too long or been punished by God. In 1954, Johann Georg Mendel's laws of heredity were a basic component of the elementary school curriculum—that two non-redheaded parents could have redheaded children could be deduced from the yellow peas, which, being dominant, allow only for the production of green peas as "grandchildren." Although my parents and us four redheaded sisters were not forced to endure a superstitious world, there still remained the suspicion of extramarital involvement: not our dark-haired father, but the redheaded postman, the milkman, indeed any of the flotsam and jetsam roaming the streets in the fifties was suggested as a possible cause of our glorious red hair. Perhaps this seemingly never-ending, almost sinister mystery surrounding the birth of redheads is the product of male fantasy: since the nineteenth century redheaded women have no longer been hurled into the fiery depths of hell but it would seem they are now forced to endure purgatory for their dissolute behavior.

What did we do to deserve this? When we were little girls we were laughed at—our freckles made us look as if we had shat on a fan, our heads resembled a burning match, a flashing fire alarm or the fat top of a carrot. They used to like to shout "carrot-top" or "witch" after us and thought they were being friendly when they called us "Pippi Longstocking" (Translator's Note: Pippi Longstocking, a young, redheaded little girl, the main character of a series of children's books by Astrid Lindgren.)—but who wants to look like the ugliest girl in the history of children's literature? Then suddenly, all this ceased to exist. Scarcely having left the scourges of childhood behind, the hunchbacked witch is transformed into a man-eating vamp. Her head still spinning from this sudden metamorphosis from ugly duckling to femme fatale, the redheaded girl stumbles over eroticism and is amazed by what she finds. What's all this about? One minute an object of derision, now an object of desire? You need a little time to get used to your new role. But then: seductive, erotic, capricious—why not? As a redheaded woman, you quickly learn how to exploit this cliché, thereby lending it credence, too. Hurt men, disappointed by their own psychological projections, augment the image: redheads are unfaithful, underhanded, dishonest and immoral. But a childhood overflowing with the taunts of others has taught us how to defend ourselves. We are rebellious, defiant, incorrigible and recalcitrant—pale Madonnas who might strike at any moment. If someone starts rubbing us up the wrong way, we become unfriendly, cold, standoffish and difficult. For we need to protect our fragile hearts from people's unreasonable demands, just like we need to protect our sensitive skin from the sun's rays. This is what makes redheaded women such unpredictable beings, so strong, and yet so fragile.

Perhaps the source of people's fascination lies in the fact that redheads are a minority. When something is alien it creates both a mysterious as well as a threatening effect. If somebody stands apart from the crowd through a shock of red hair instead of the usual ash-blonde, or through a myriad of freckles instead of a uniform tan, then they exert an enticing effect. But they also instill fear. Can such creatures even be trusted? How does such a person think, feel and act? In the past, this xenophobia has claimed lives among redheads, although accounts of scores of redheaded women being burned at the stake are a largely over-exaggerated myth of the nineteenth and twentieth centuries. Here our fascination for beauty in the midst of horror has caused these allegedly dangerous women to be recast in the smoldering role of Lucifer's very bride. But the redheads were victims of poisonous tongues, their reputations have always suffered. Christianity made all of its dubious biblical characters into redheaded scoundrels— Eva, who paved the way to worldly suffering, Salome, who murdered without cause, Judith, whose intentions were more honorable but who nonetheless committed atrocities, Dalilah, who swindled an innocent man. Then there was Judas, the epitome of the underhanded redhead. Herod slaughtered innocent children—and he was a redhead.

In order to escape this evil legacy, redheaded women in centuries past went to great pains: their red hair was bleached, covered with salted red snail, set to with lead combs, cut and hidden underneath wigs. Freckles were subjected to a barrage of Spanish white and white lead, lemon juice, powder, quinine and "Swan's white." Yet none of it helped. For through the camouflage of respectability, the specter of the redhead's sinister reputation could still be felt. Ultimately, the women of the Parisian demimonde were able to turn the tables at the end of the nineteenth century, when they made red hair their trademark. A whole generation of poets and painters, already battered by the insurrections of disobedient women, poured forth their ecstatic adoration for these highly stylized creatures, who, at the same time, they despised. *Et Voilà,* a mystic creature comet into the world: the "femme fatale." The Symbolists and Pre-Raphaelites, Toulouse-Lautrec, Klimt, Munch and all the others ecstatically celebrated the creature's arrival yet avoid it like the plague. One hundred years later, a hair-cosmetics company summarizes concisely in a beauty manual: "All men dream of an affair with a capricious, red-headed beauty. But as a wife, they would all prefer a refreshing blonde." For in so doing, they are erring on the side of safety.

Thus, life is not, and was not, so easy for redheads. However, we suffered our greatest defeat in the twentieth century. Self-confidence and pride were finally ours, we strutted conspicuously into the arena (as we had secretly probably always yearned to do) when lo, we found ourselves drowning in a sea of impostors. For the first time in history, there was a demand for red hair on the heads of headstrong women—and a cosmetic industry quick to respond was capable of supplying all the Evas and the Salomes with all imaginable shades of red. Now that is really mean. The only small consolation is the fact that a true connaisseur is still able to distinguish the genuine article from all the frauds: the fair, freckly skin, the headstrong, uncompromising nature and the impatient, belligerent temperament.

Plates

**"Everybody was so excited at Fanny's birth,
and they all wished for her and us
that her hair stay the same color."**

Anne Jung, Fanny's mother

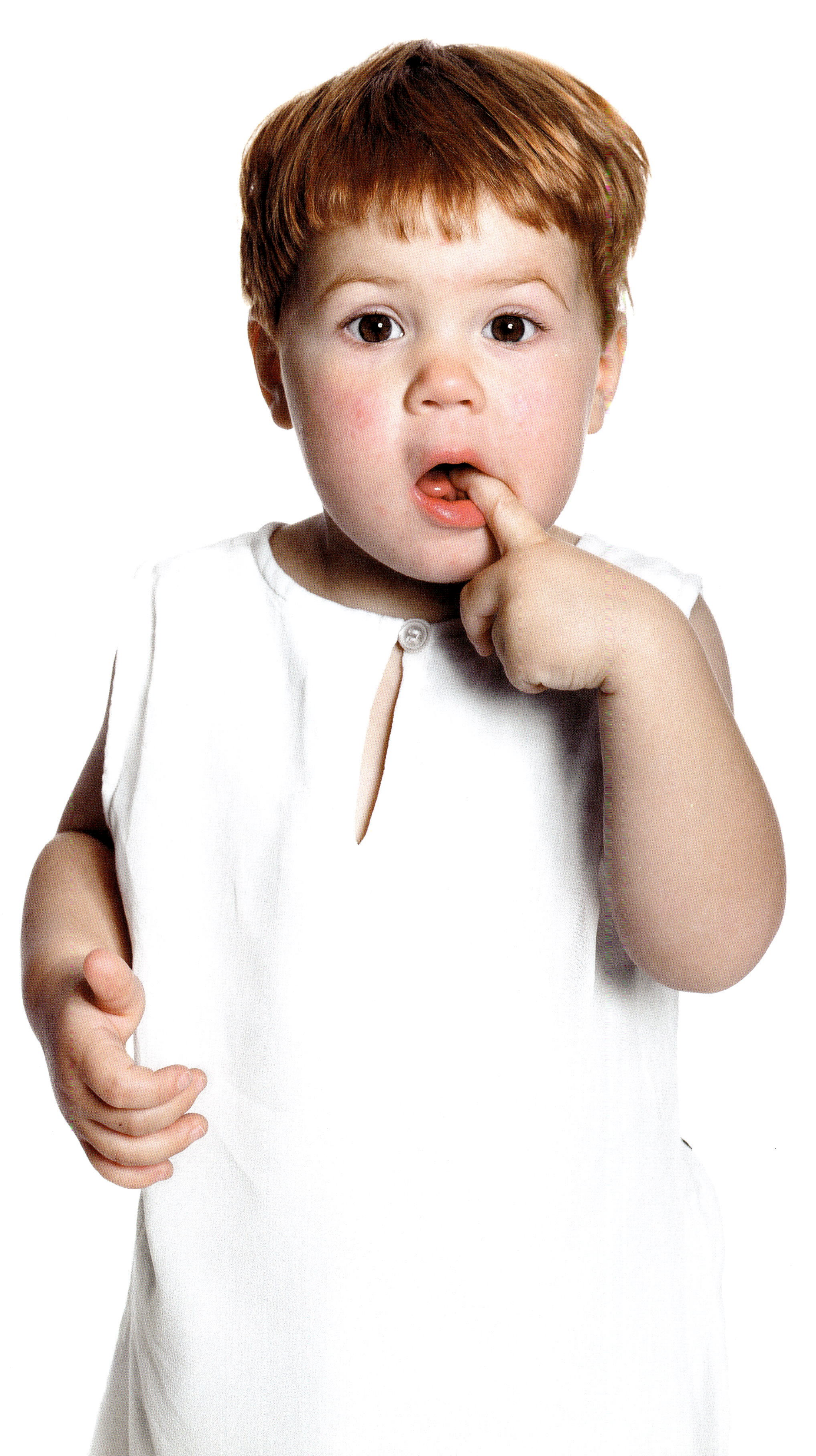

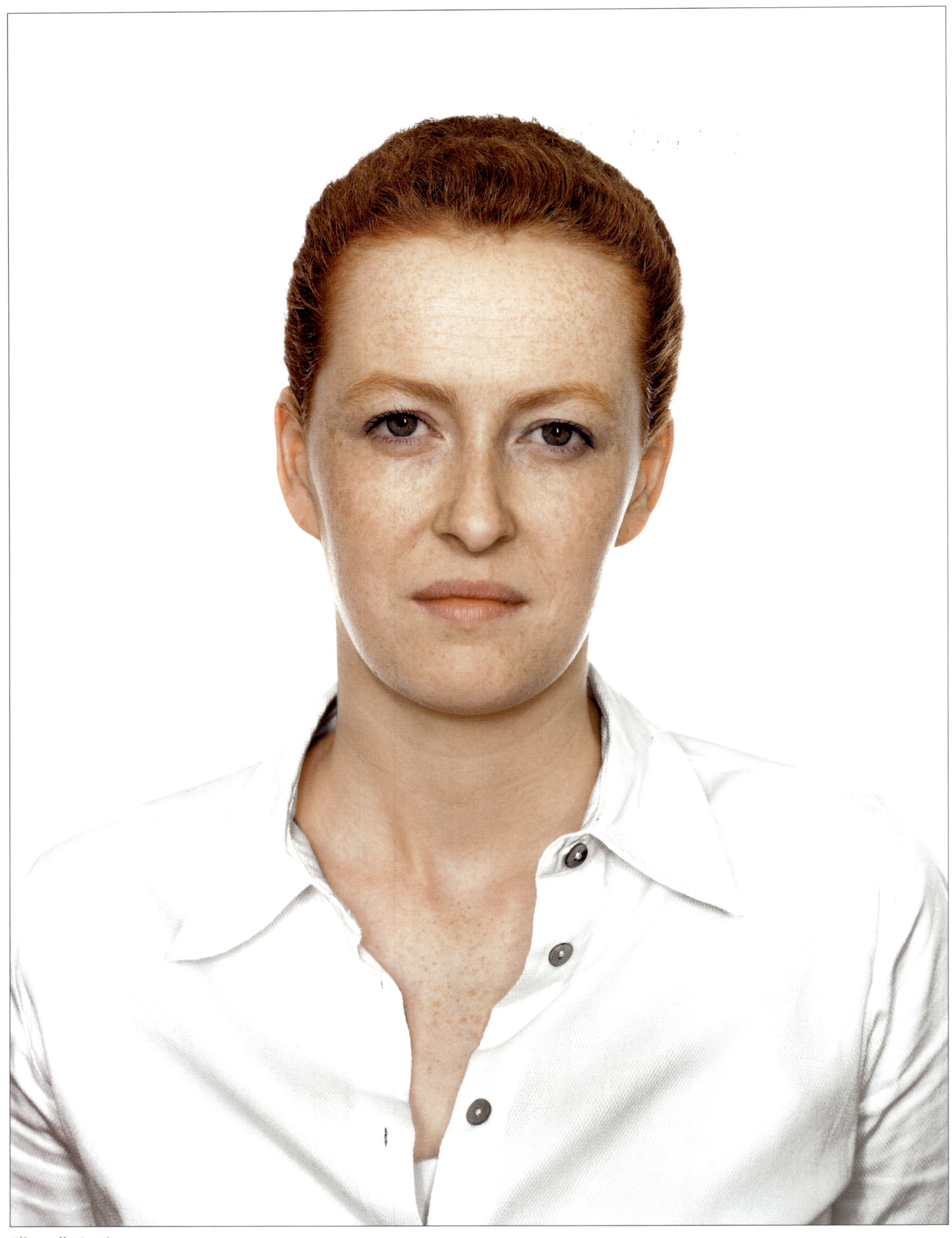

Clionadh Curtin

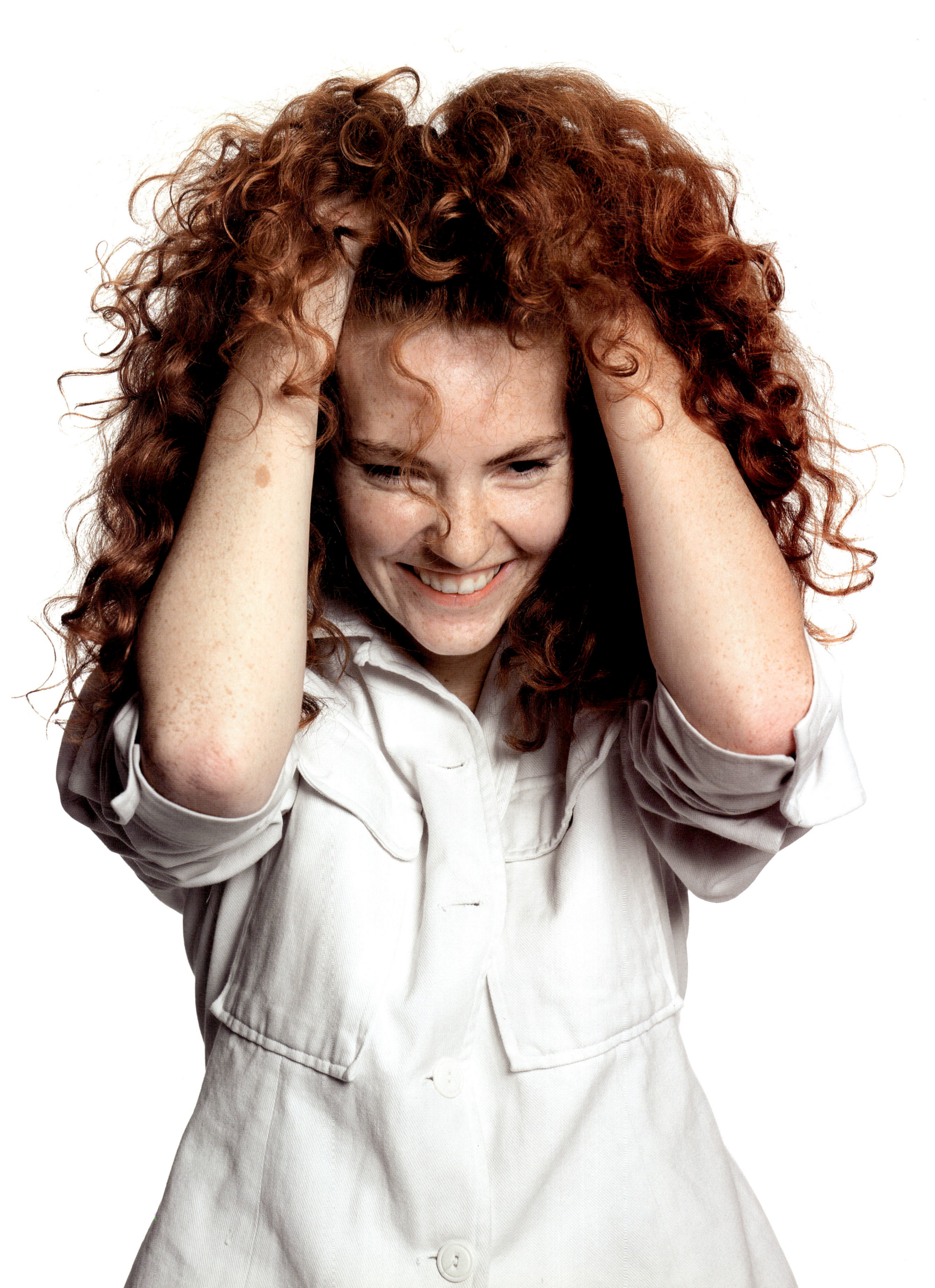

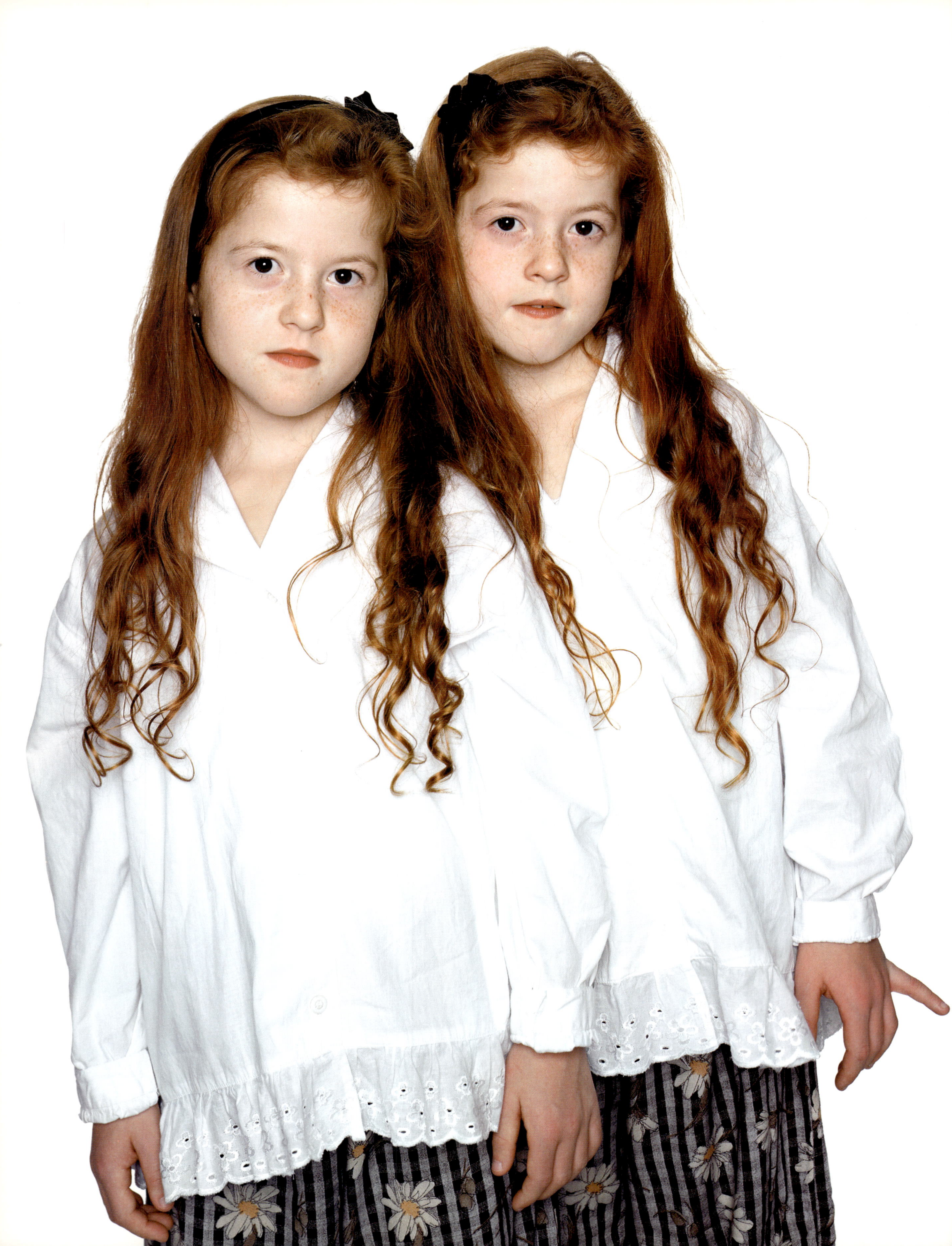

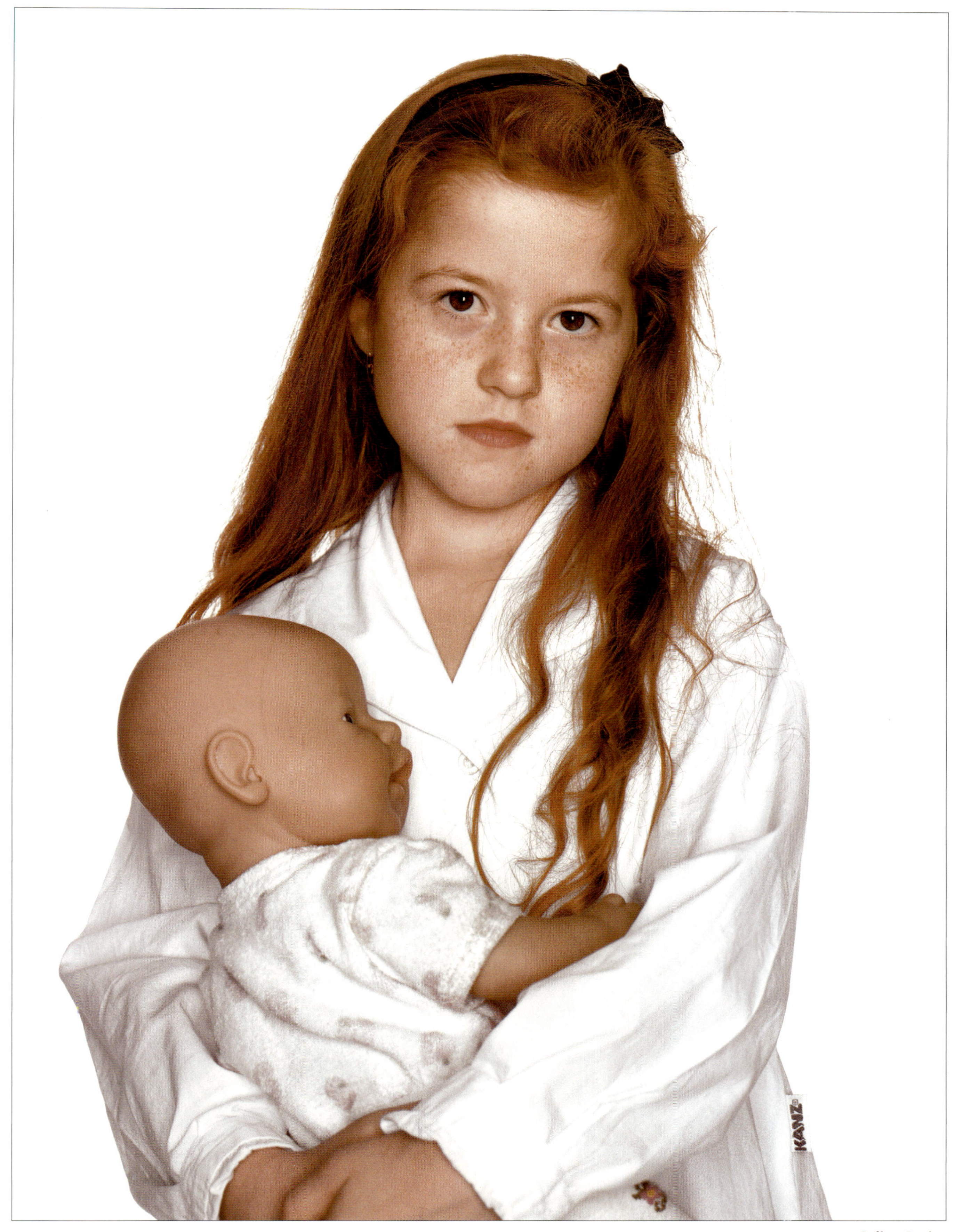

Selina Breier

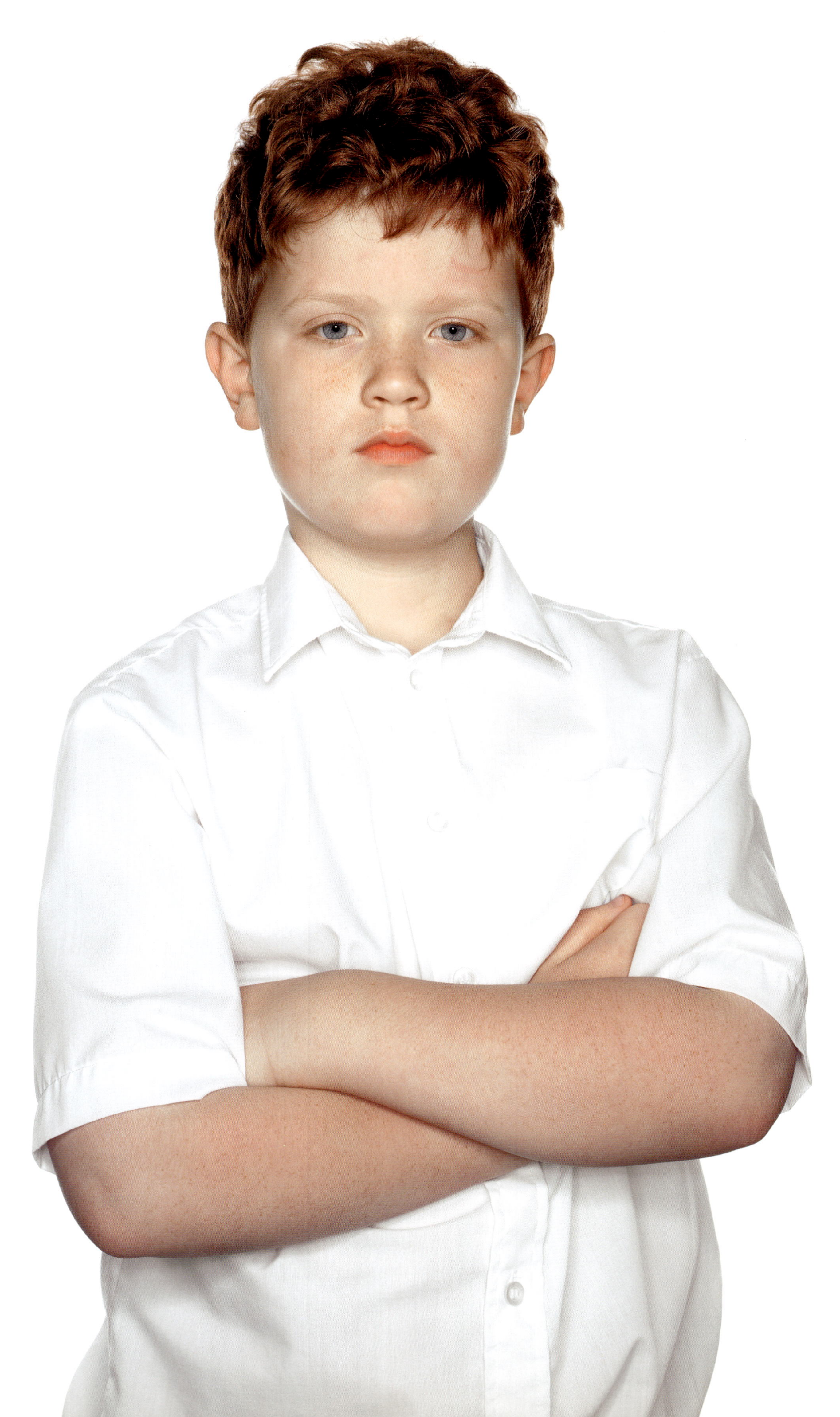

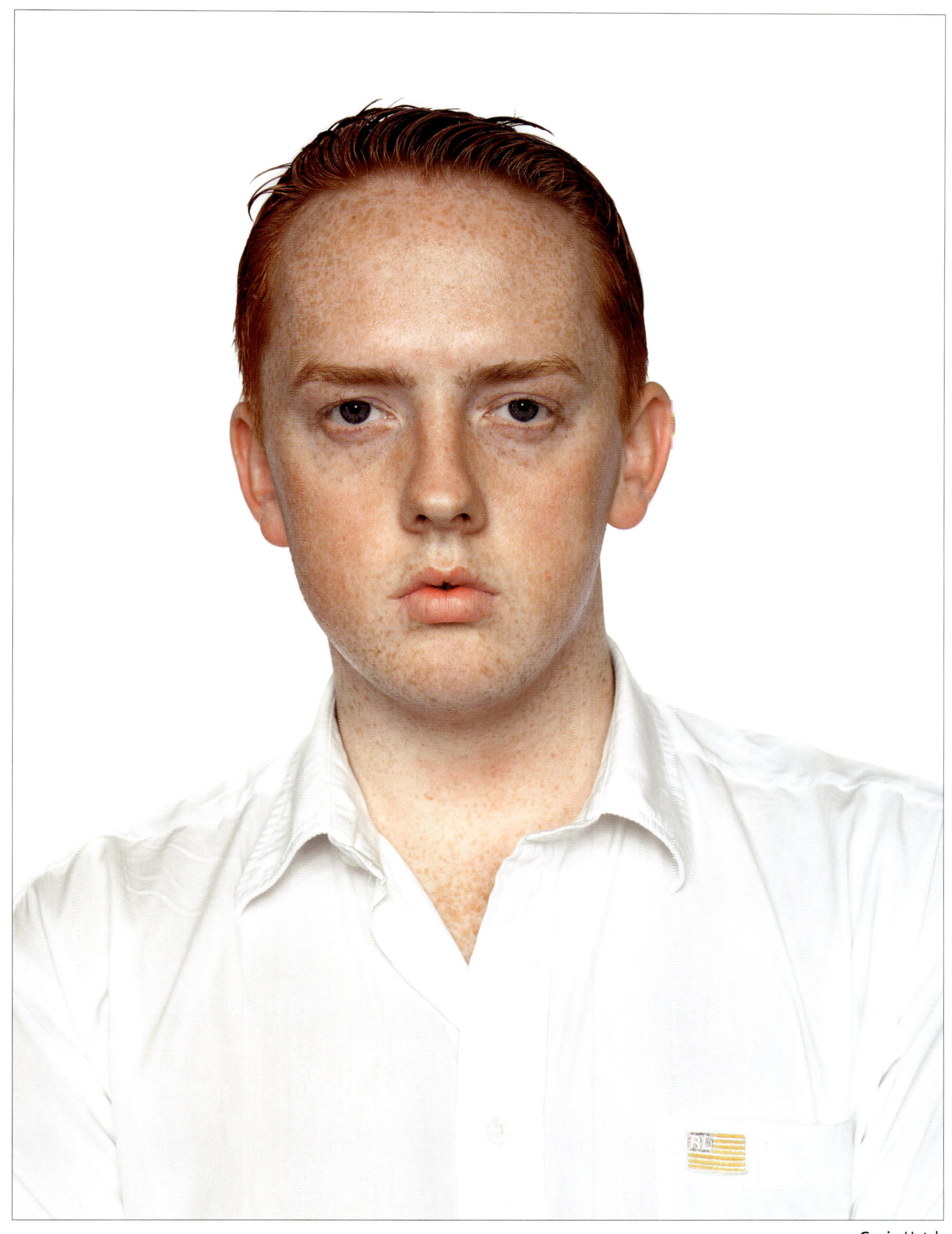

Gavin Hatch

"As a kid it wasn't very nice having red hair.
Now I look back and laugh
because it is nice
being that little bit different."

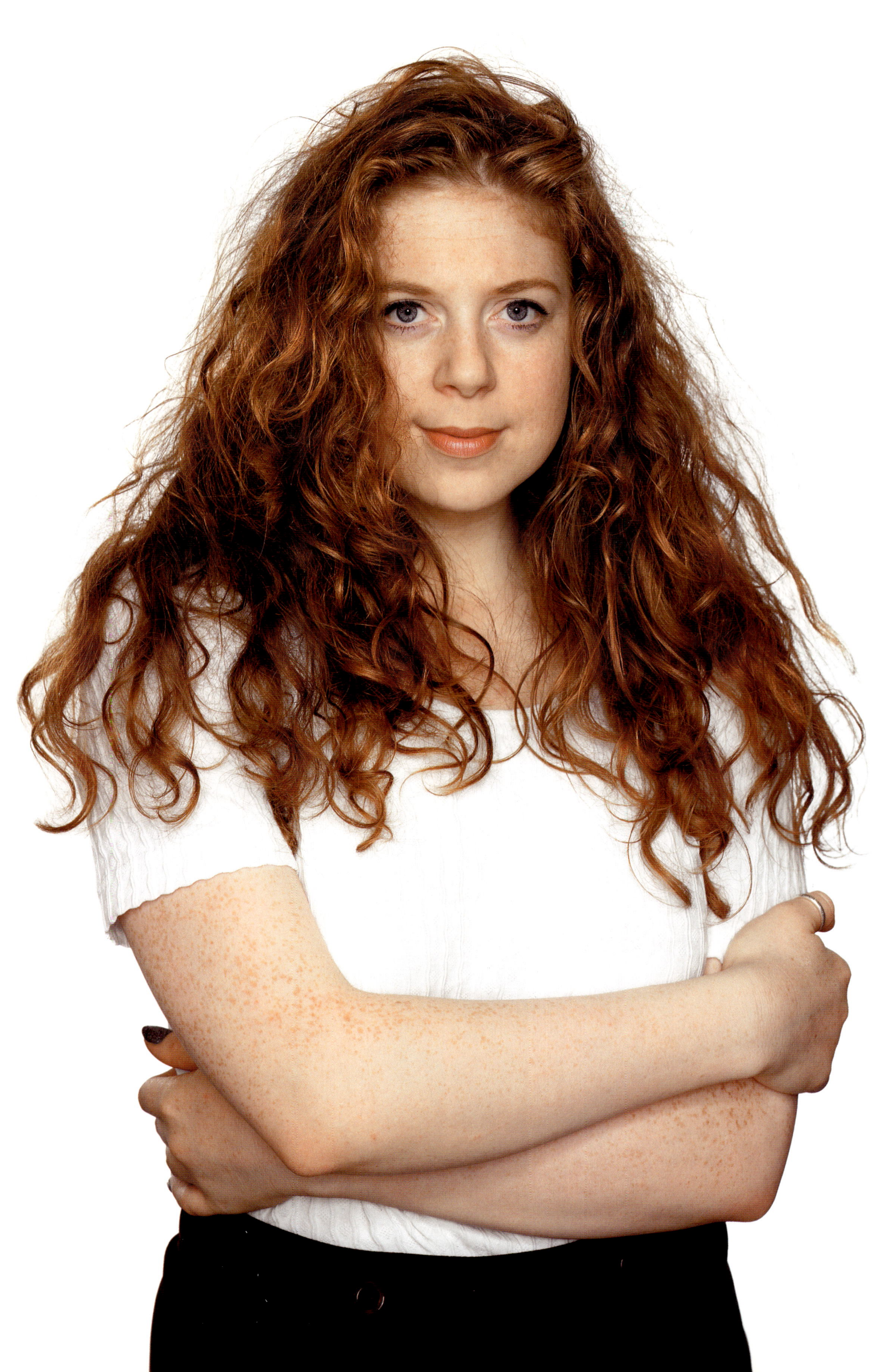

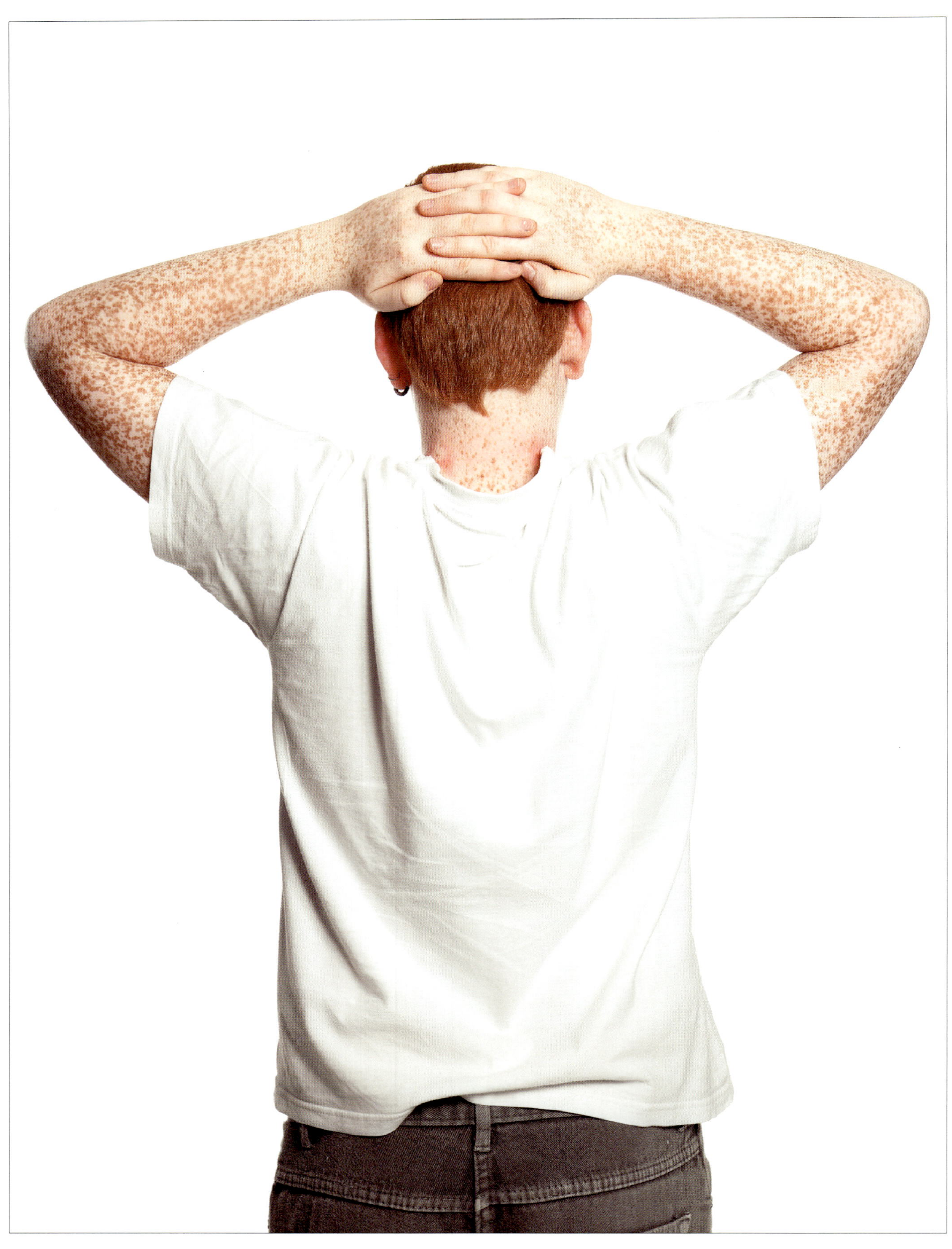

Anton Borisow

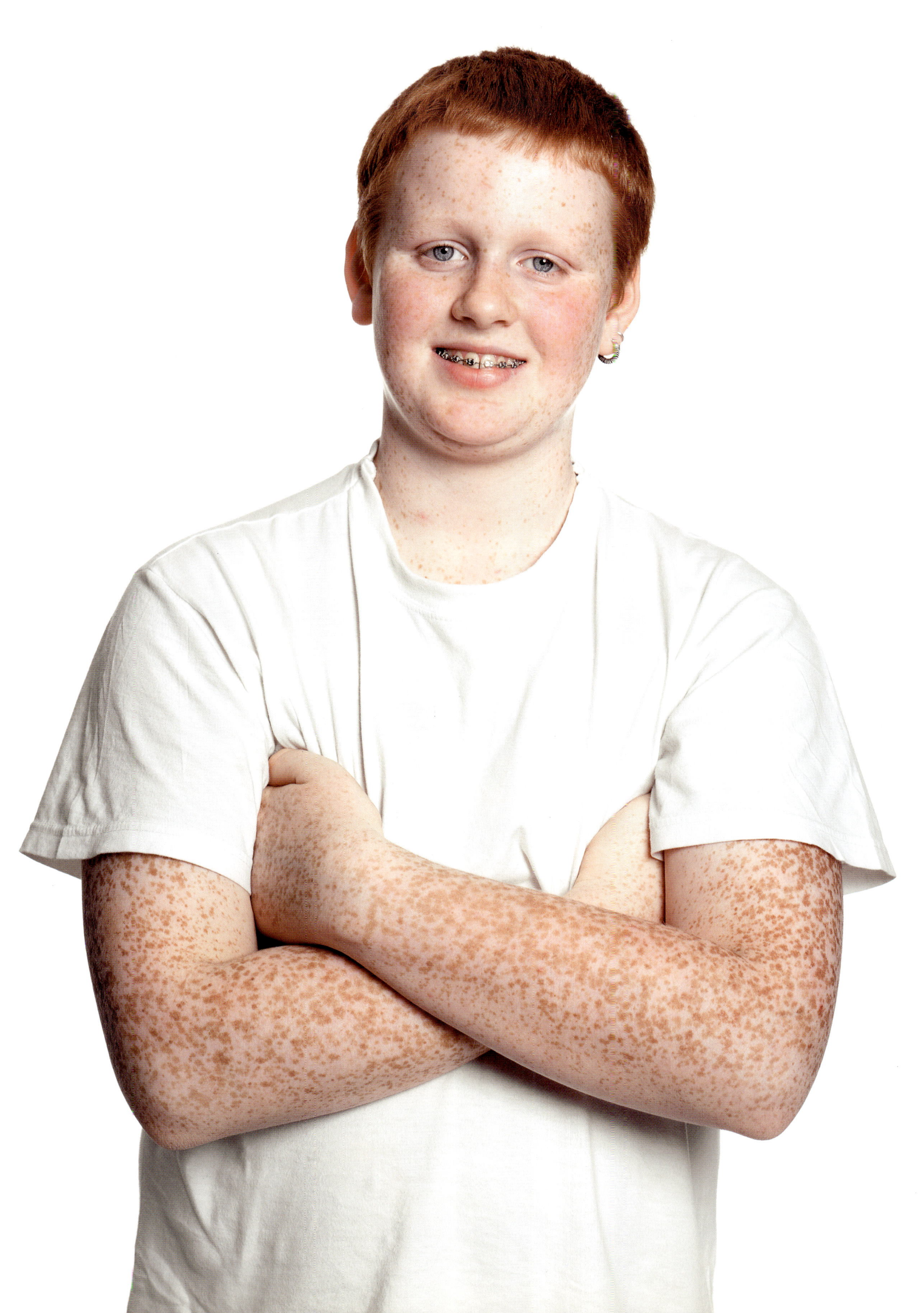

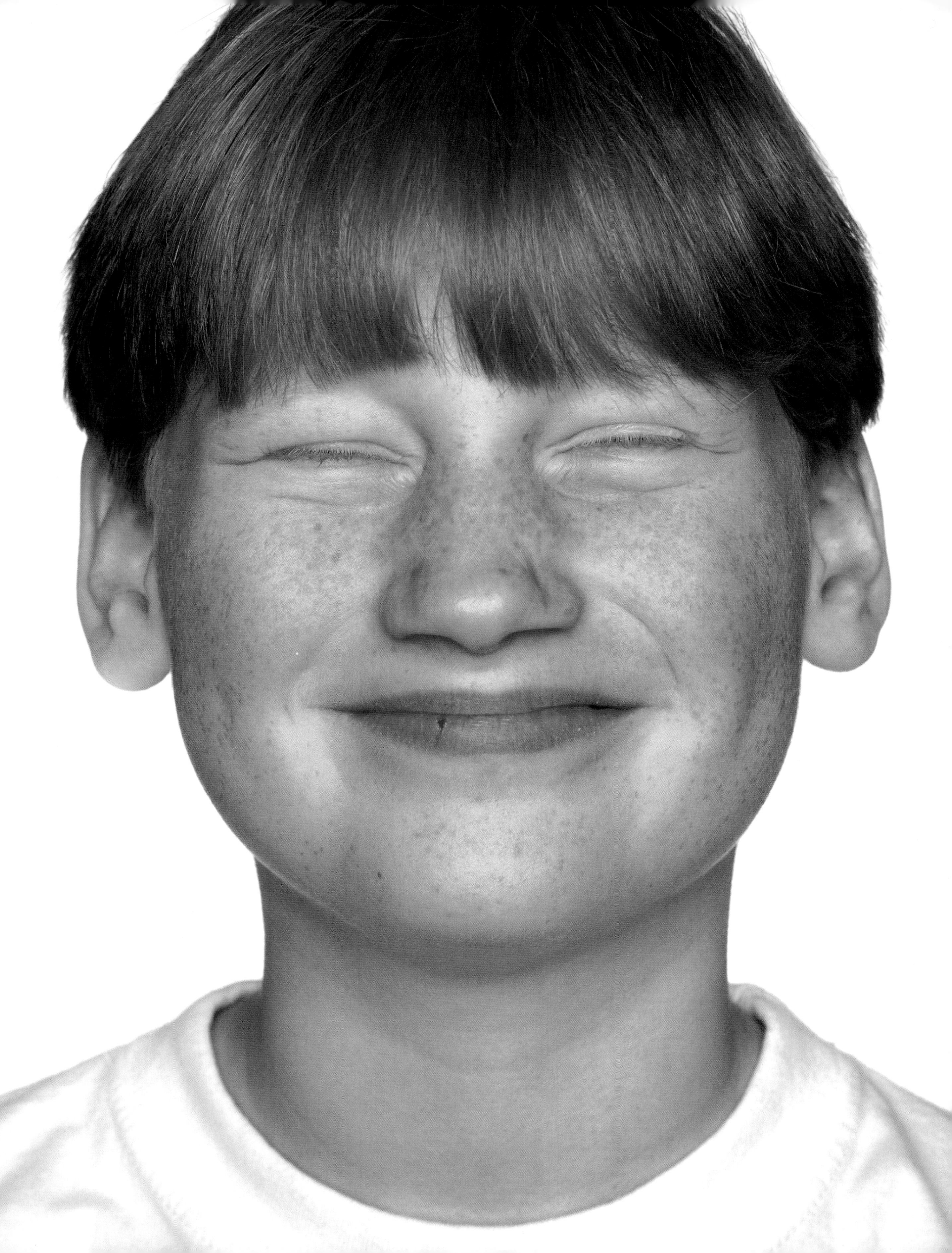

"I'm beginning to realize
that redheads
are extremists by accident."

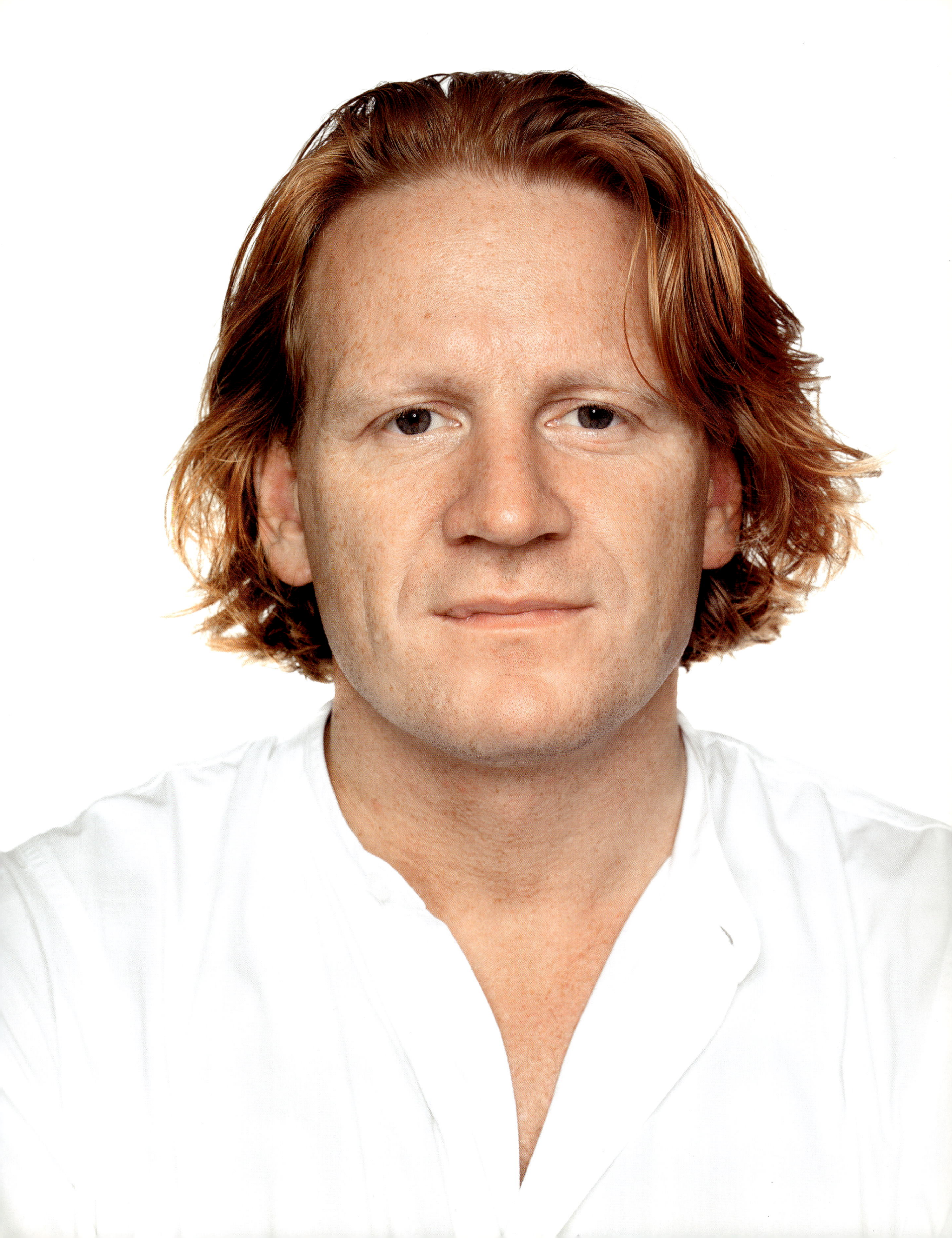

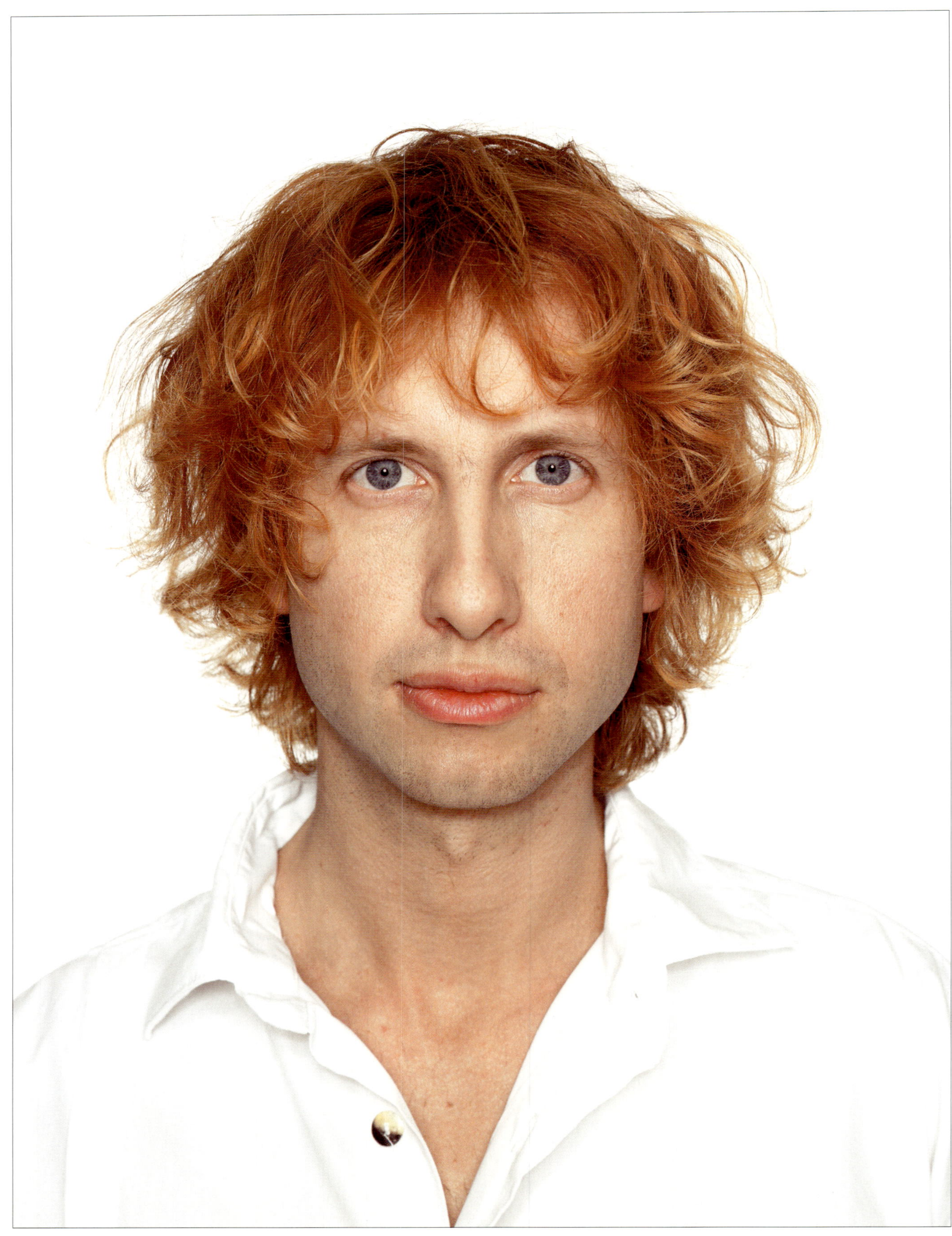

Nicolai de Treskow

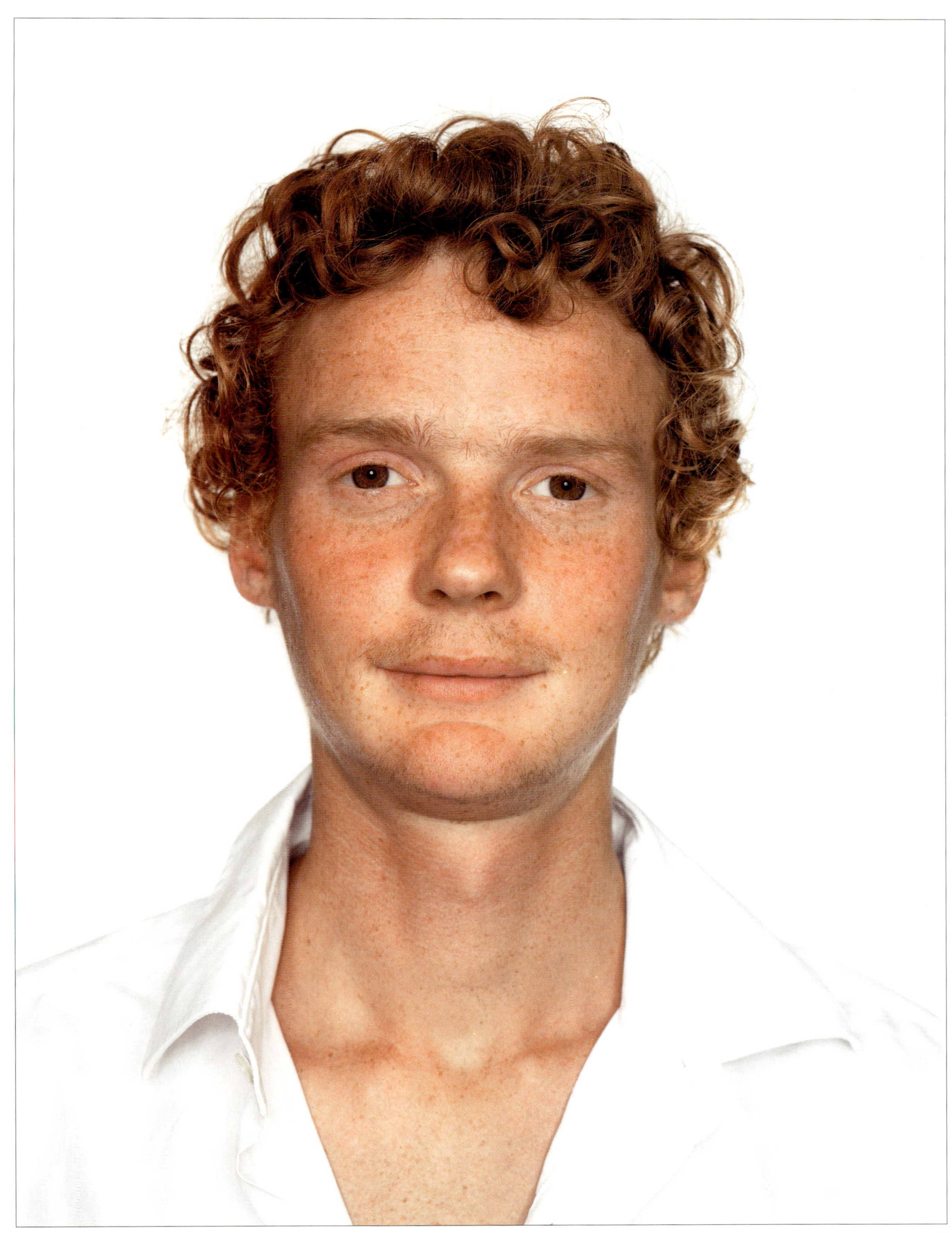

Killian Driscoll

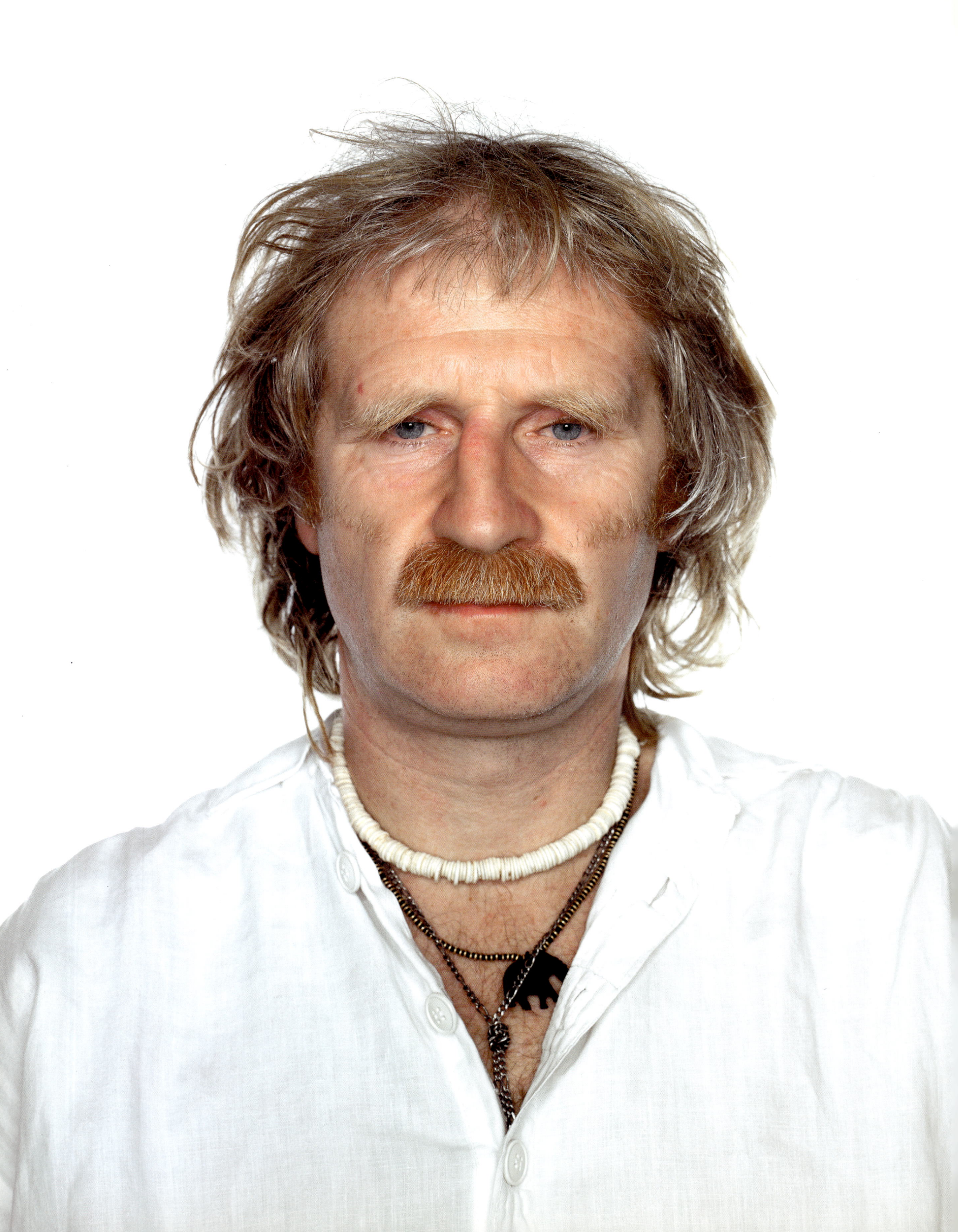

"Being noticed is,
when interpreted correctly,
a very positive feature
in one's life and increases
one's self-awareness."

"Where did you get that hair?"
one American wanted to know.
"It's born." "Oh, it's burnt? That's cool!"

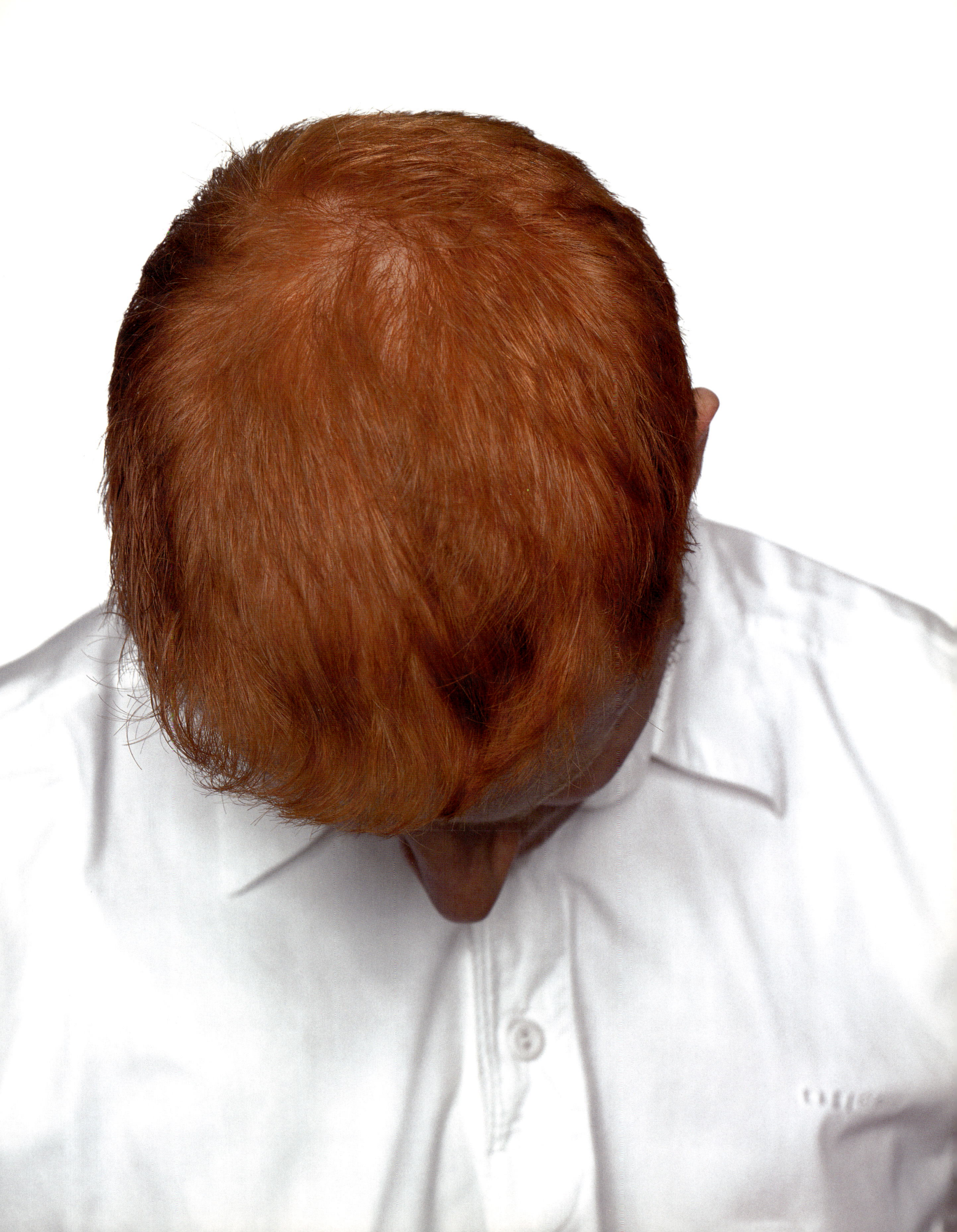

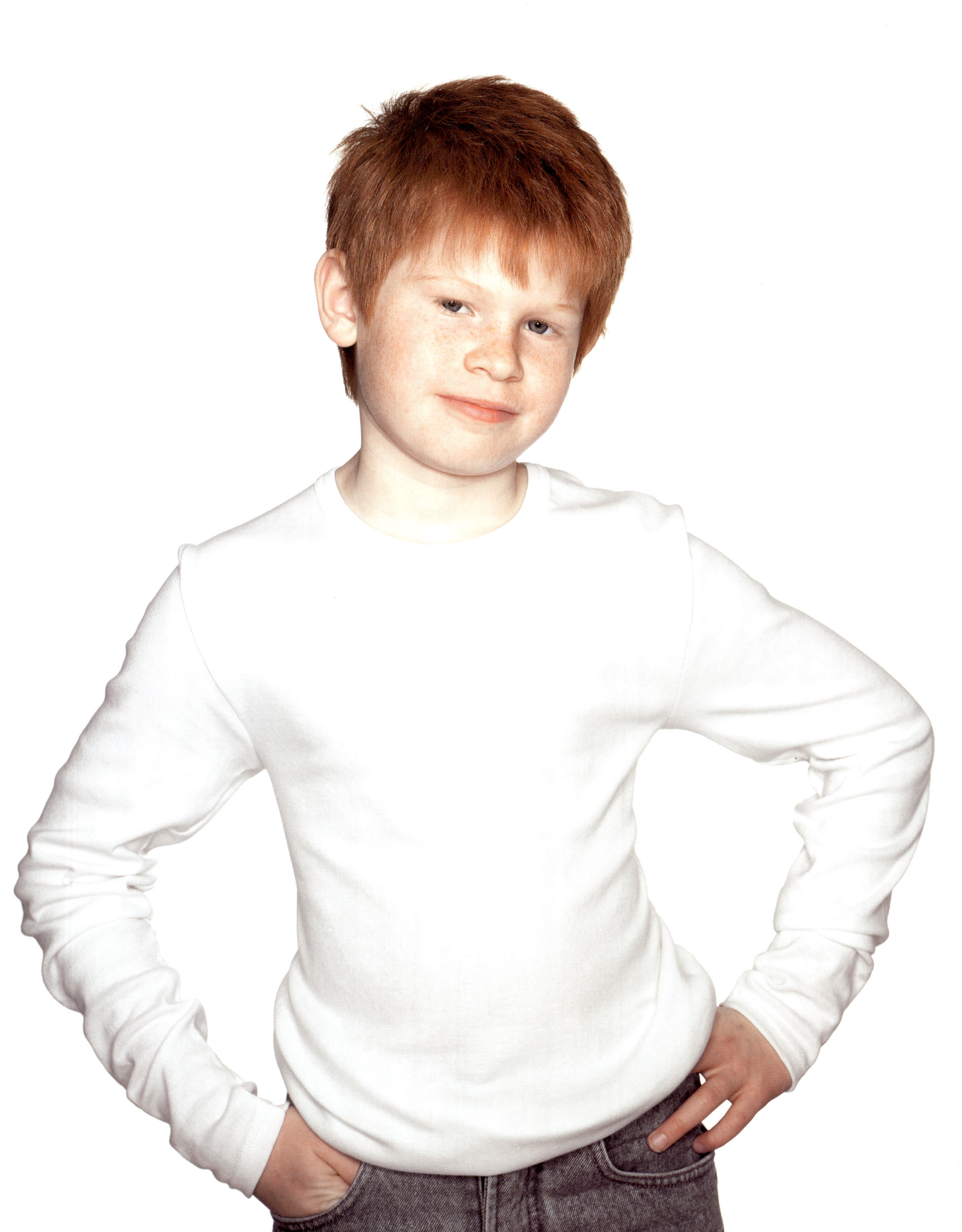

"I always tell people
about the way I used
to play Irish harp music
when I was pregnant with Felix.
This is the reason
that his soul found its way to me."

Monika Krüger-Stahl, Felix's mother

"I don't even bother to trying
to get the perfect tan.
I just stick with perfect white!"

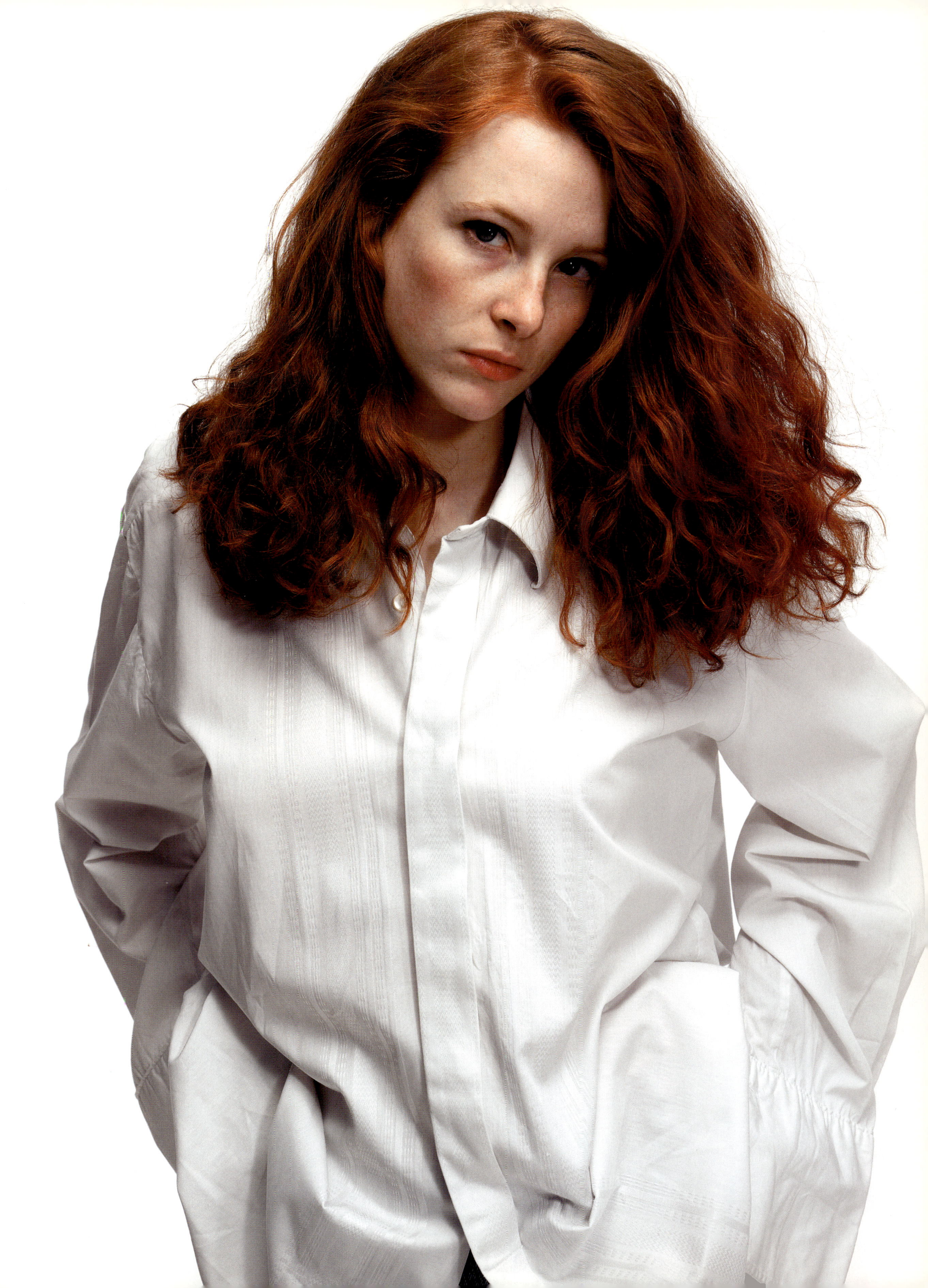

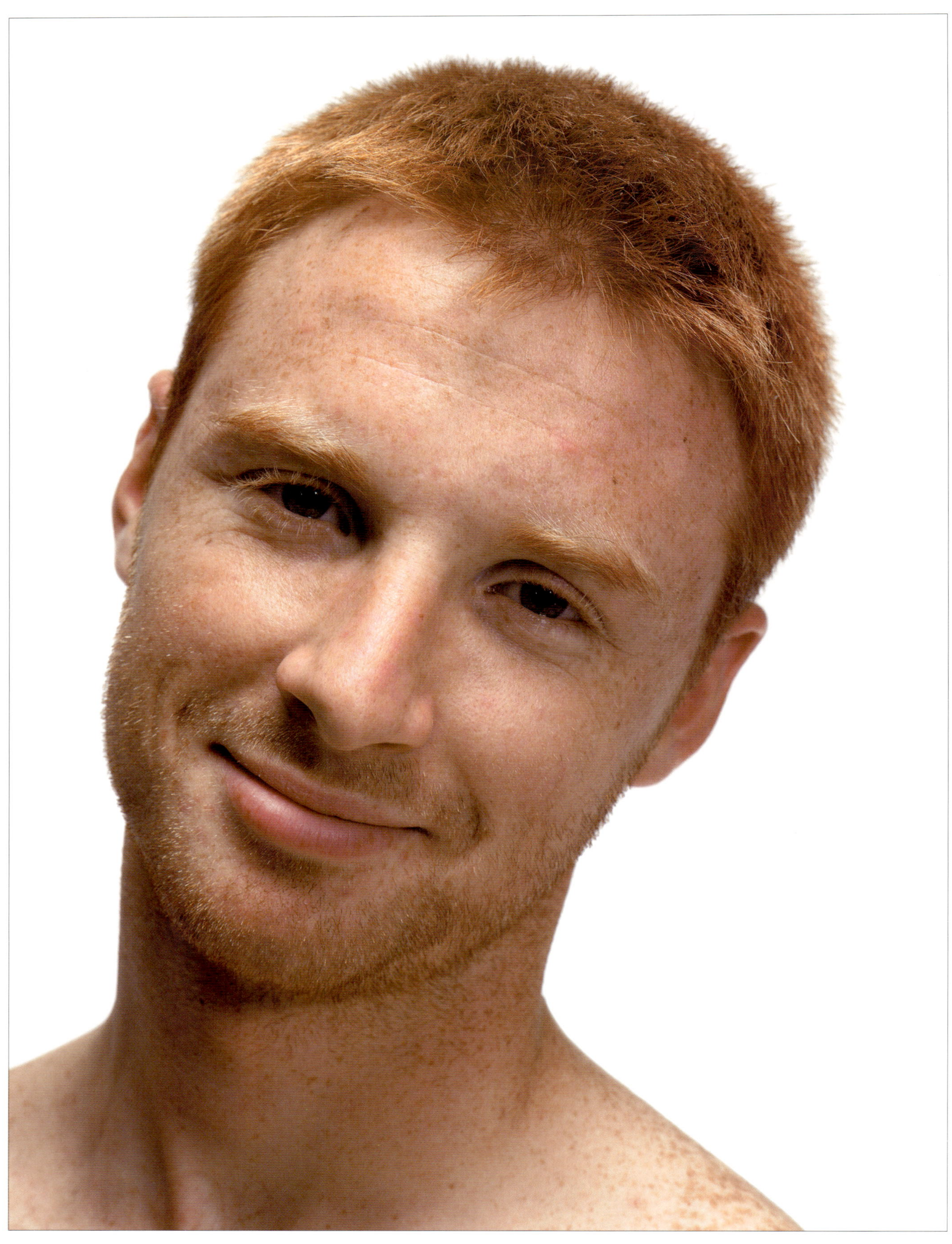

Jan Meier

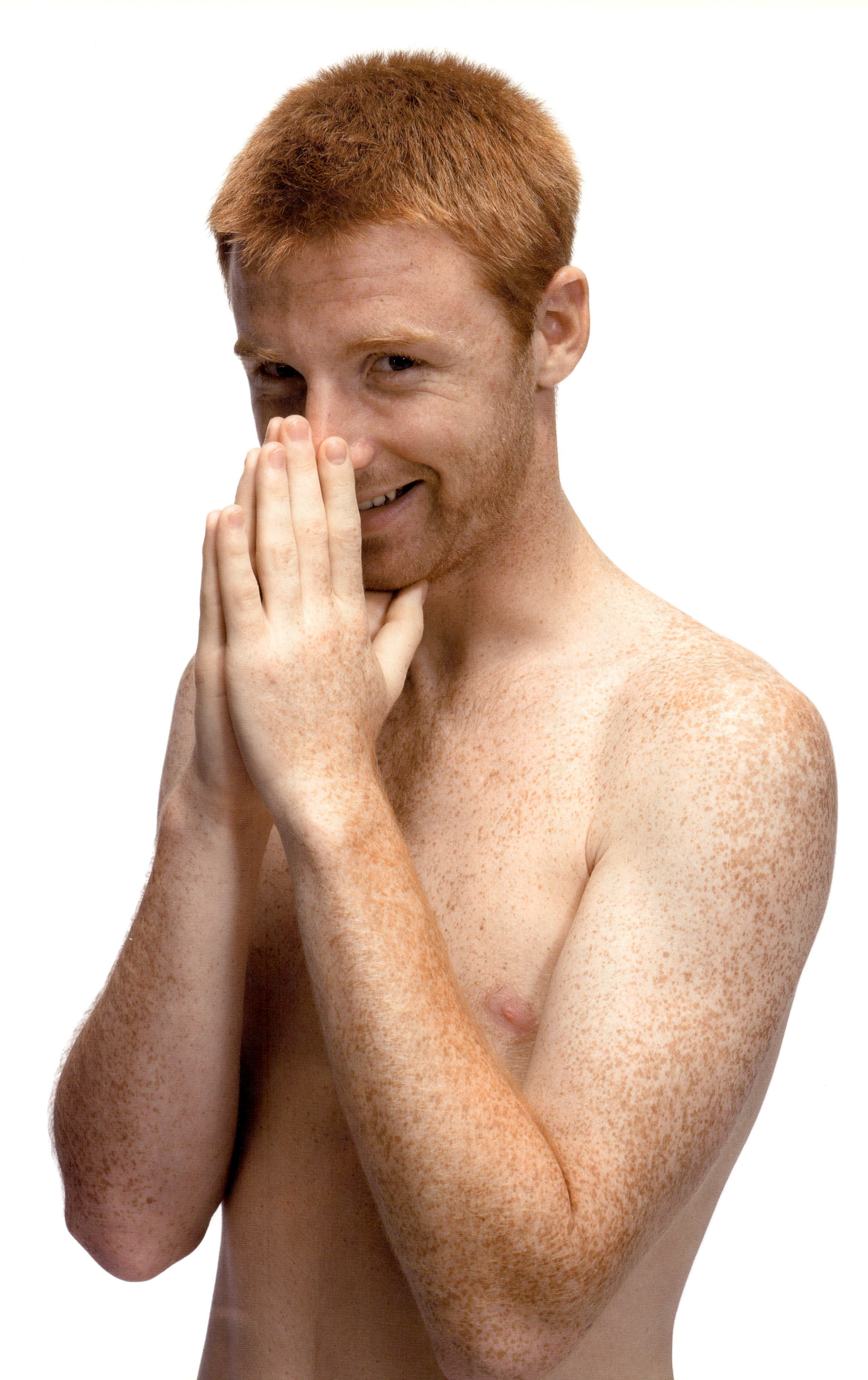

"When I was a child
I wanted to be like everyone else–
now I thank God that I'm not."

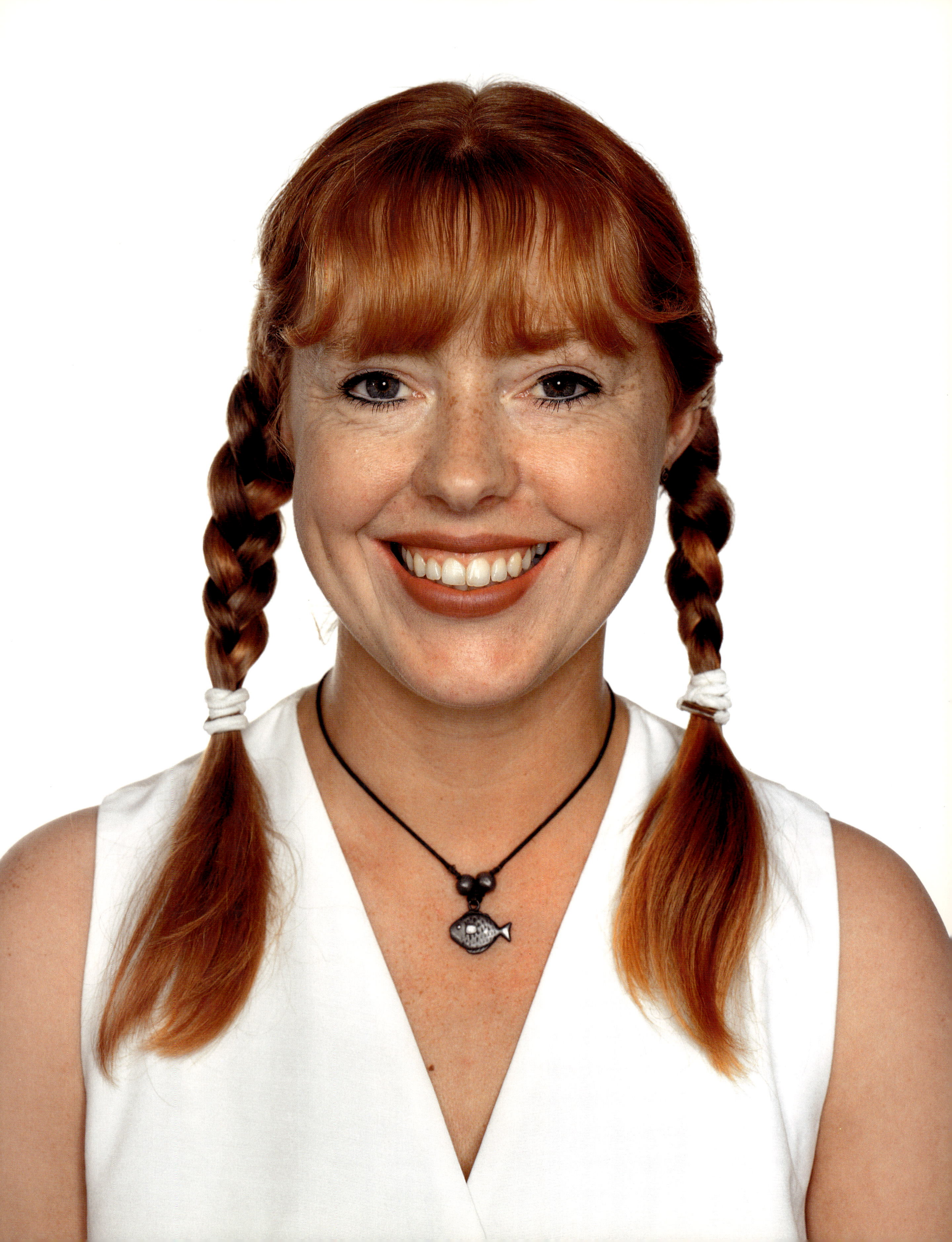

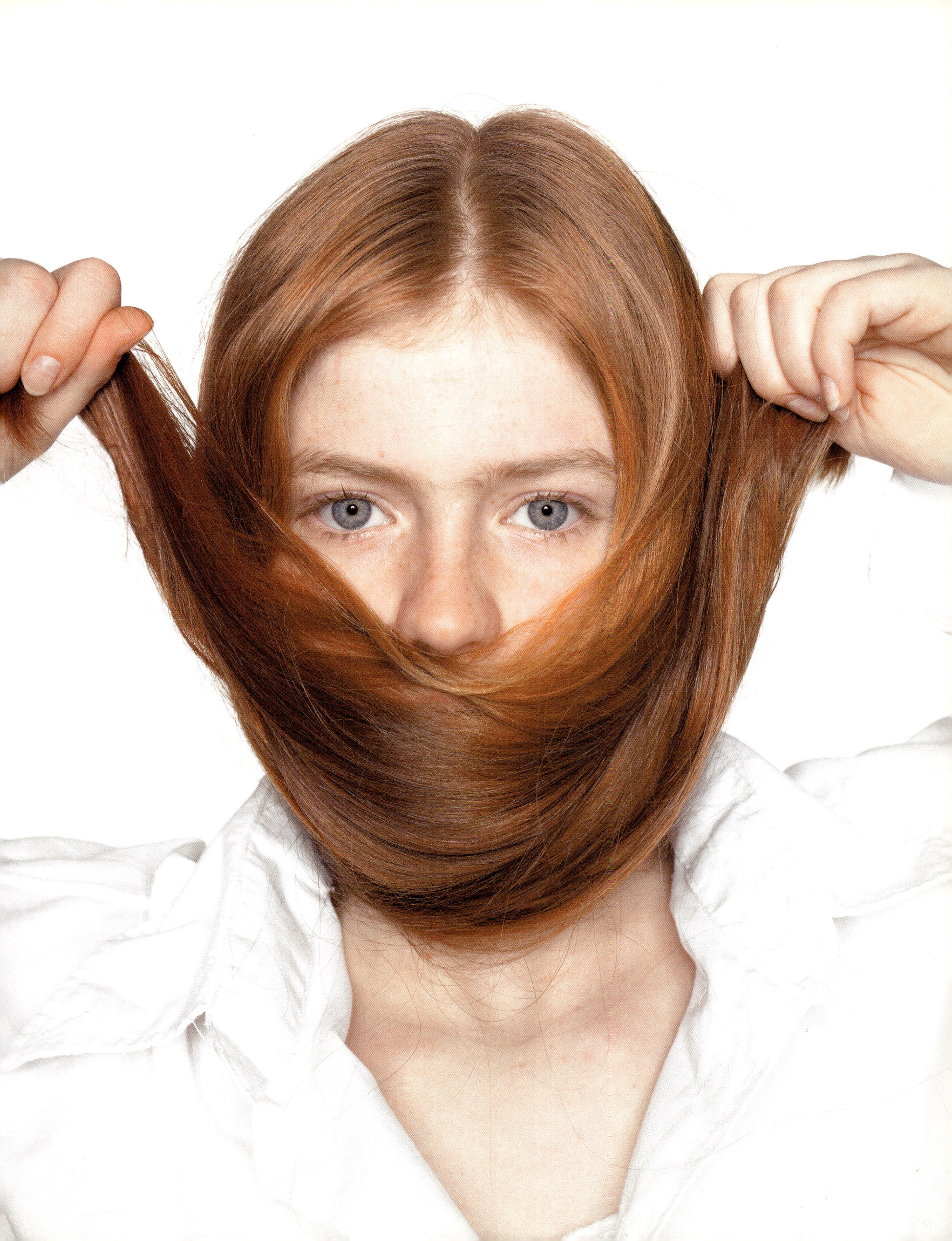

"I didn't have any problems
dressing up as Pippi Longstocking
for the Carnival.
Sometimes this is even my nickname."

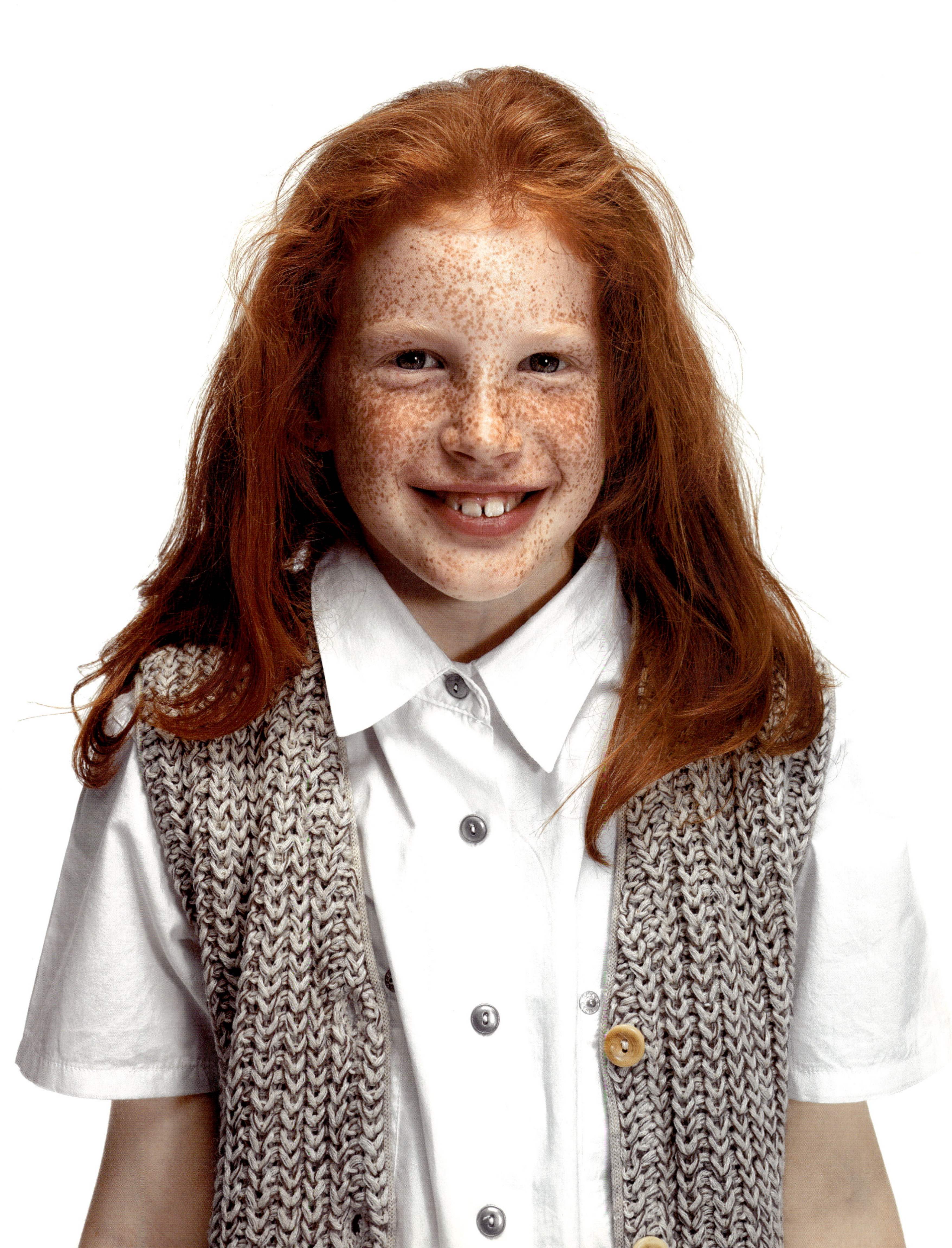

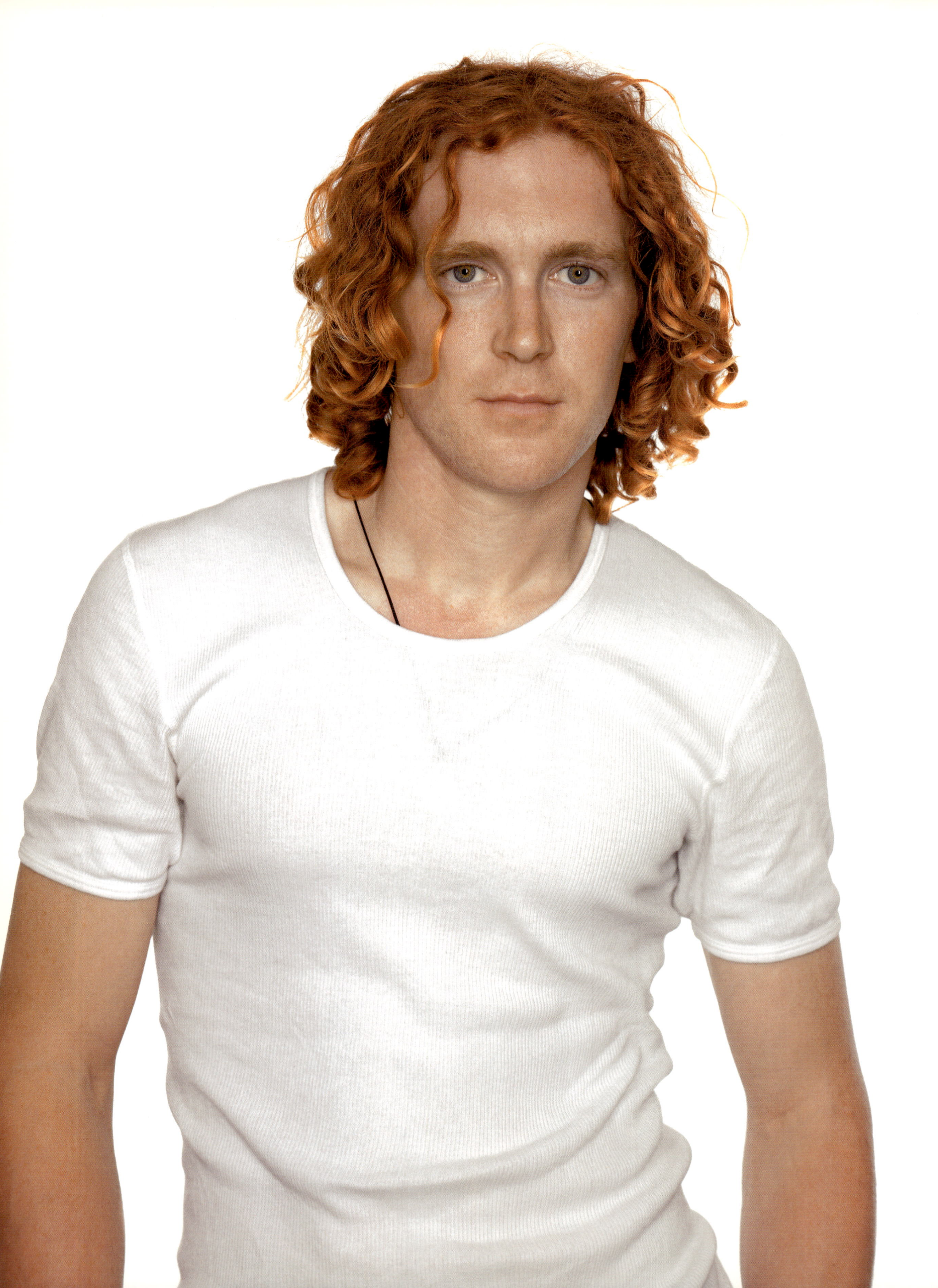

"My red hair is a celebration
of all things Celtic;
its spirituality and earthly wisdom.
It is the essence of natural beauty,
like the sound of the winds,
or the taste of autumnal fruits.
It gives me a wonderful sense
of how nature touches human presence."

"Red expresses fire,
energy, the joy of being alive and verve.
These are qualities
that everyone would like to have."

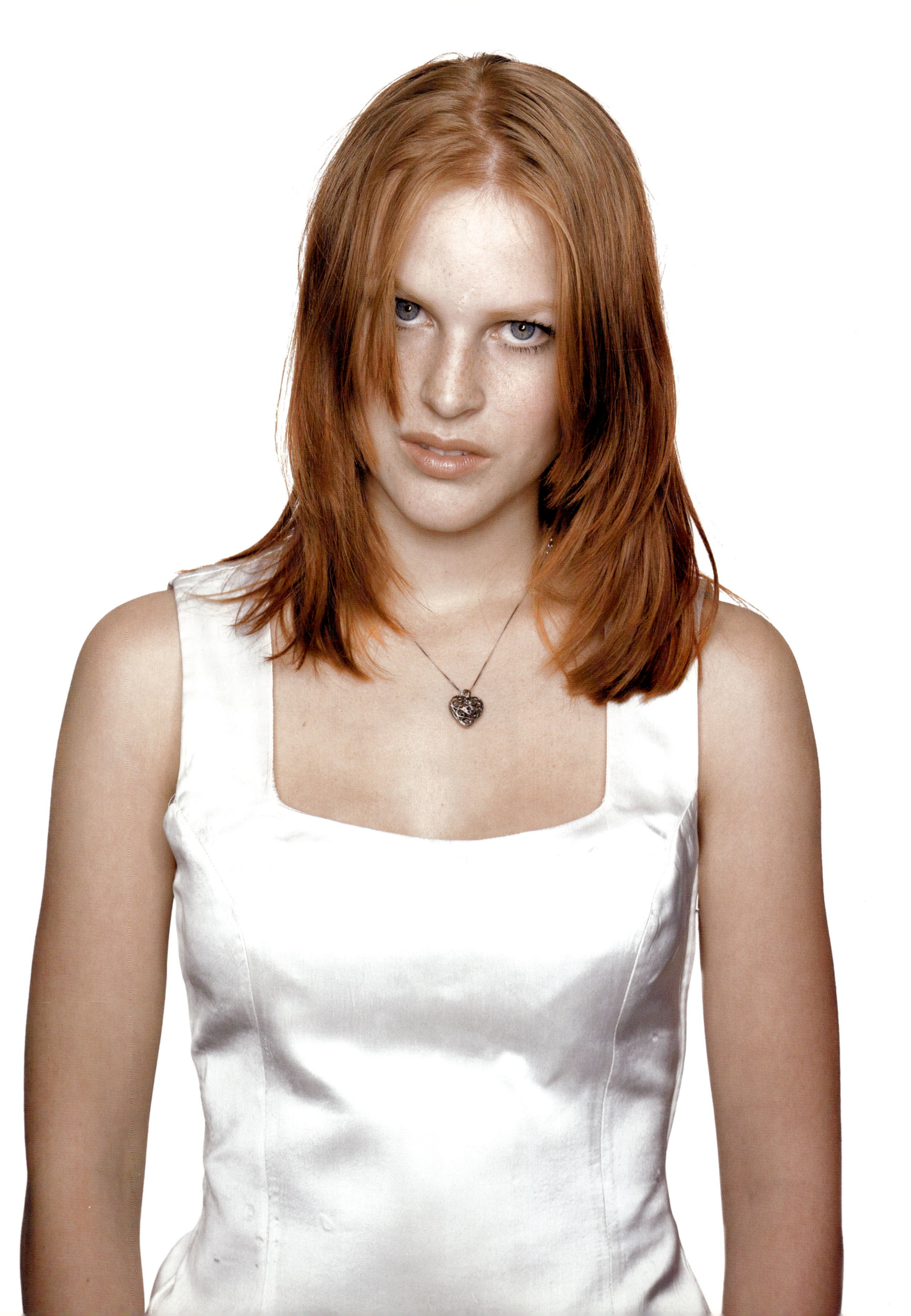

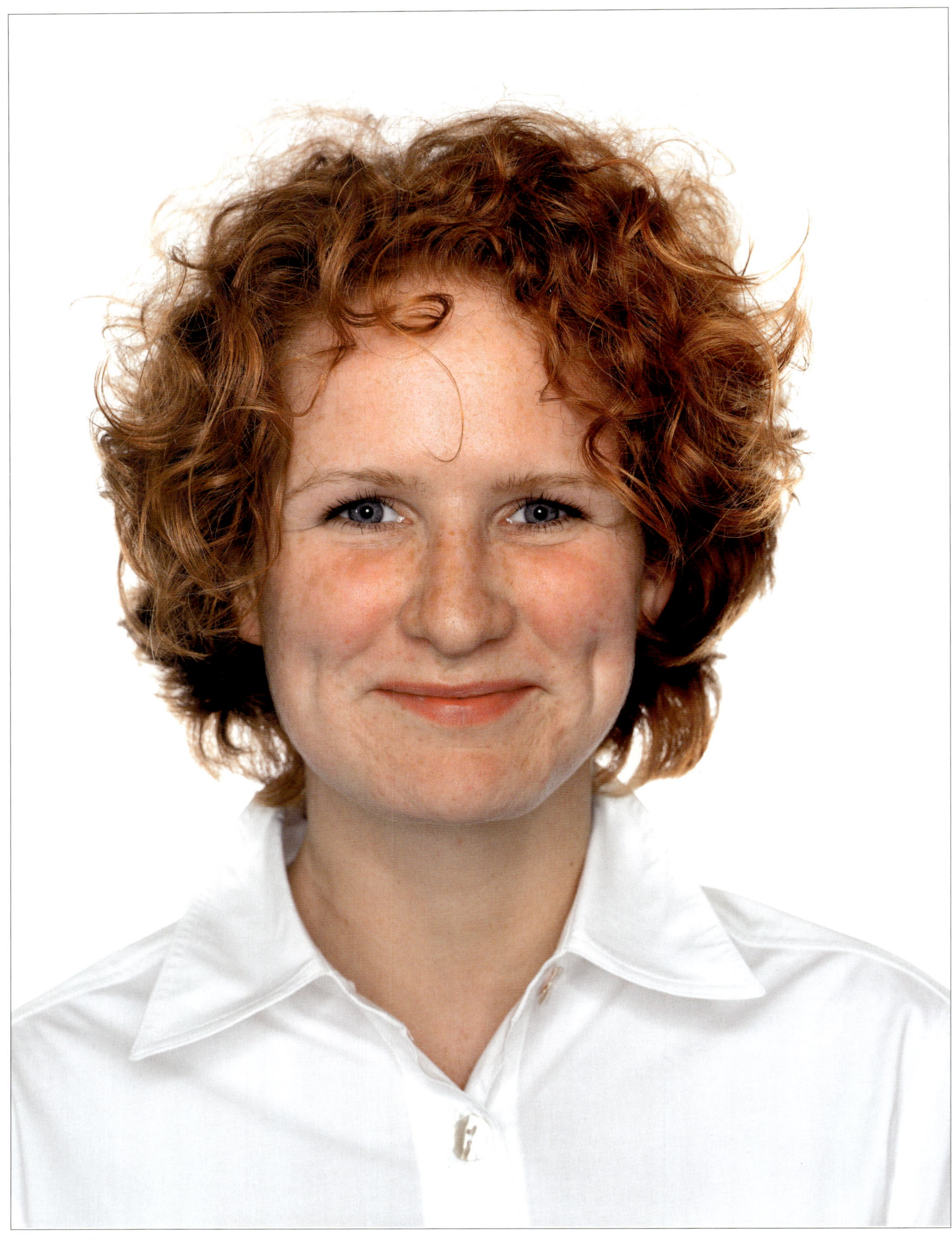

Jayne Enright

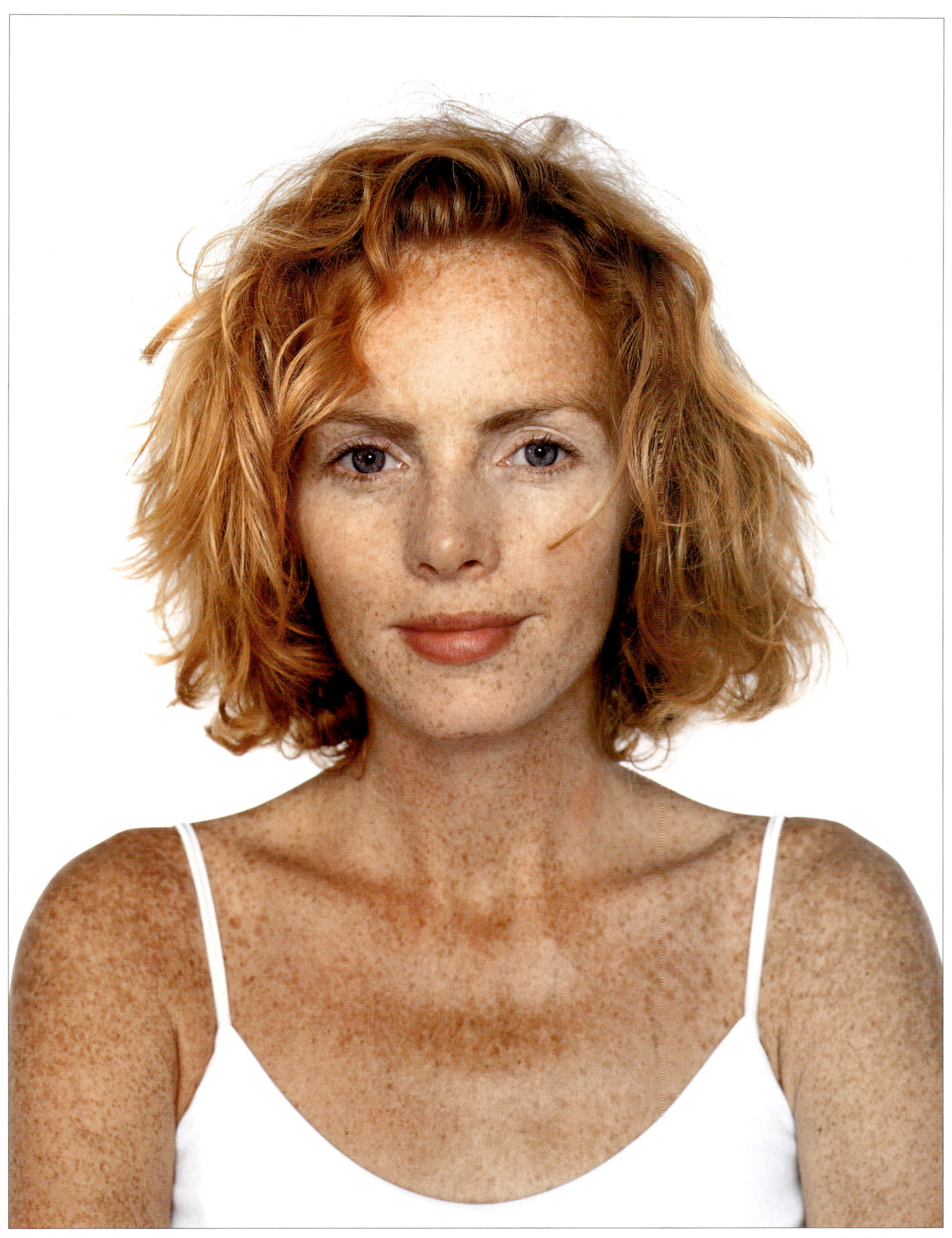

Sonja Reynolds

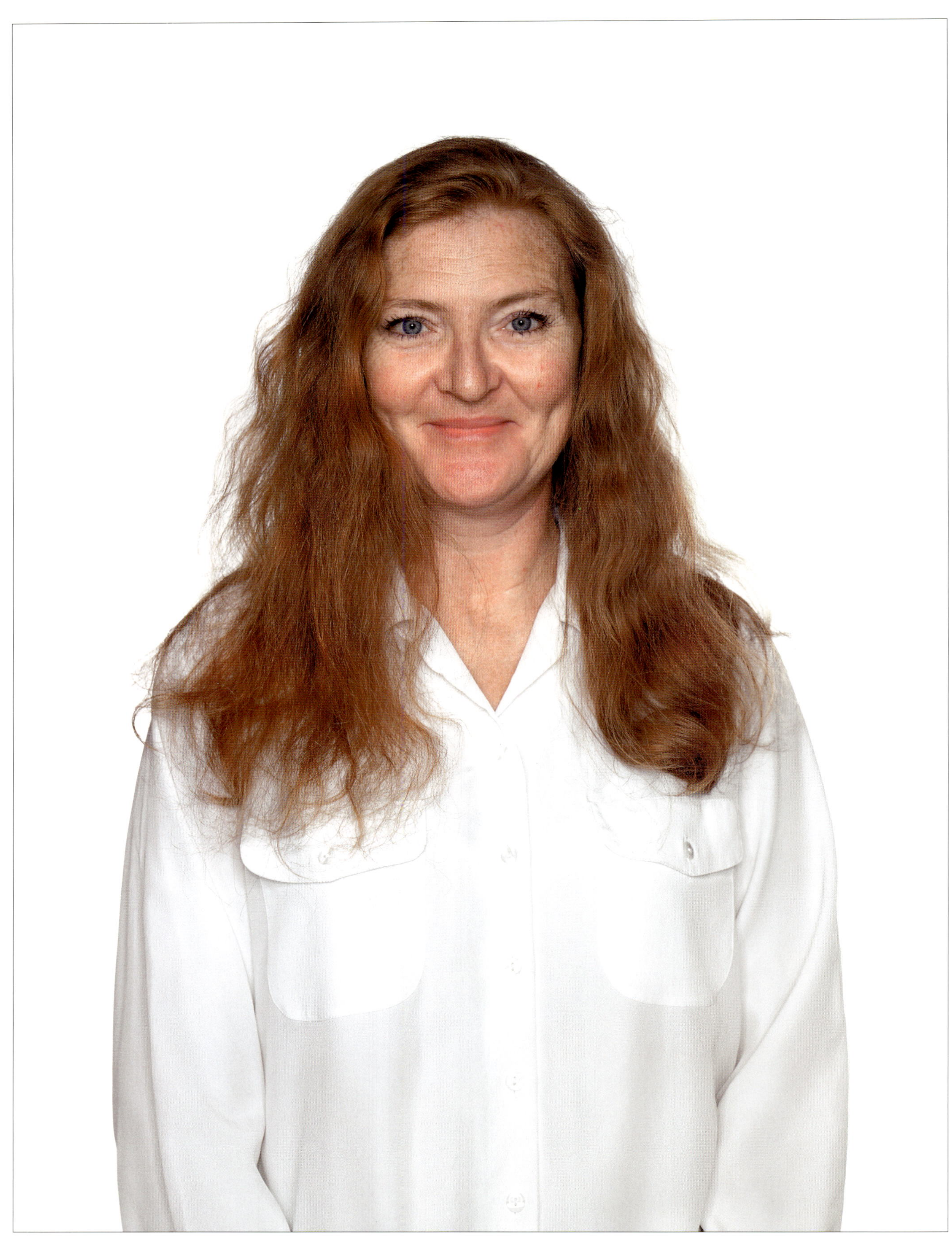

Jenny Boden

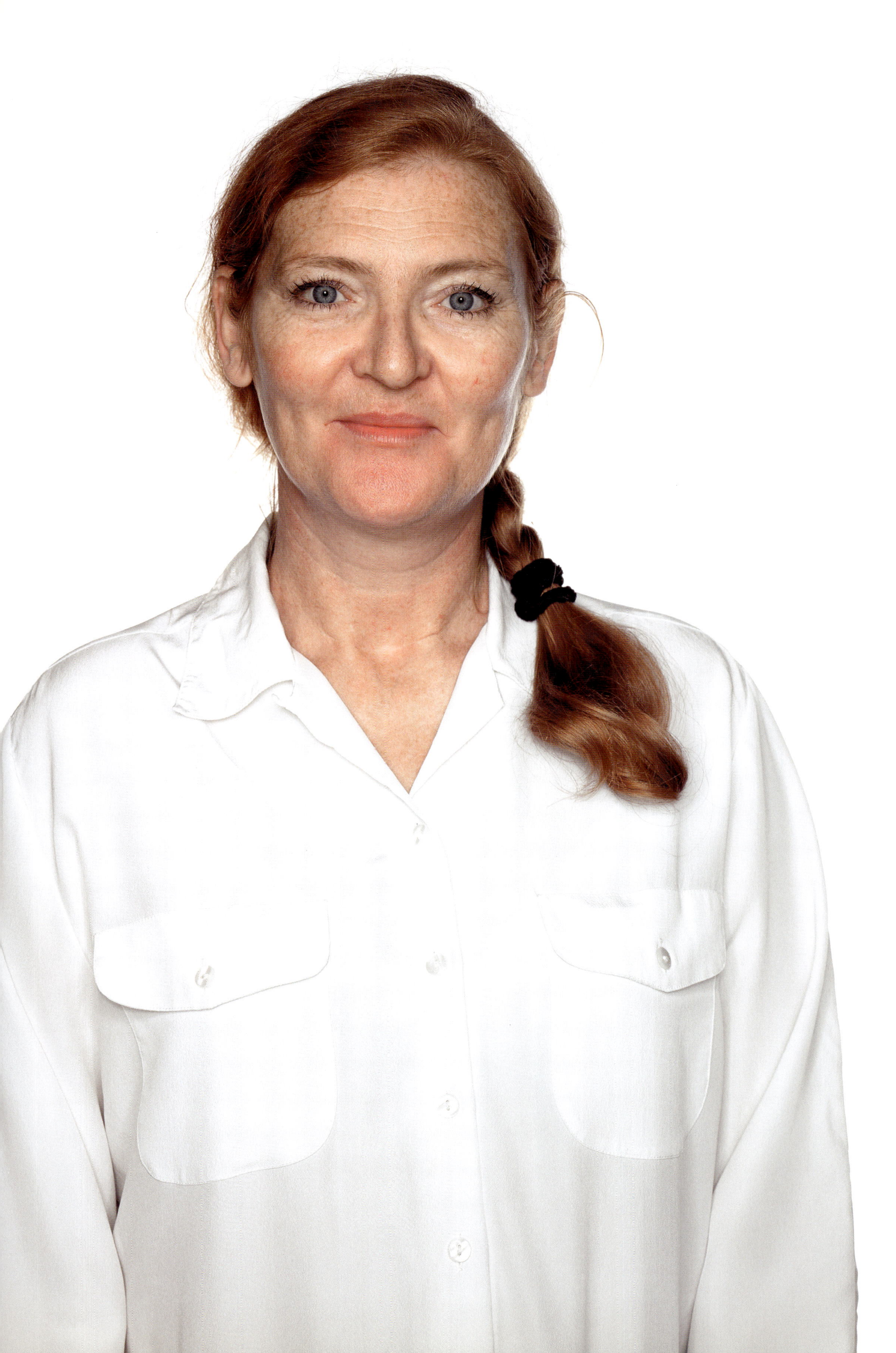

"It doesn't matter how I try,
whatever shade I want to tint my hair,
it just gets redder!"

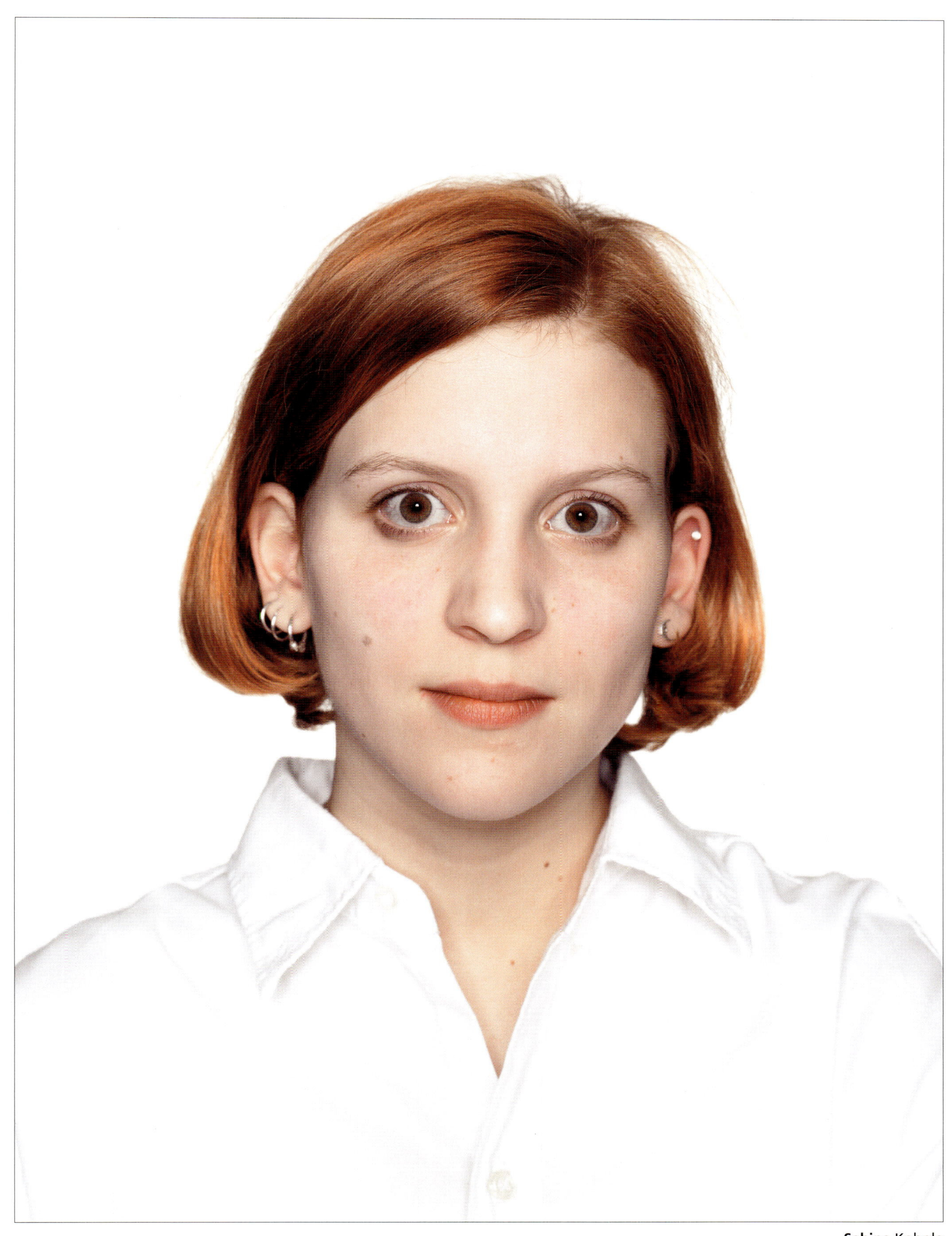

Sabine Kohnle

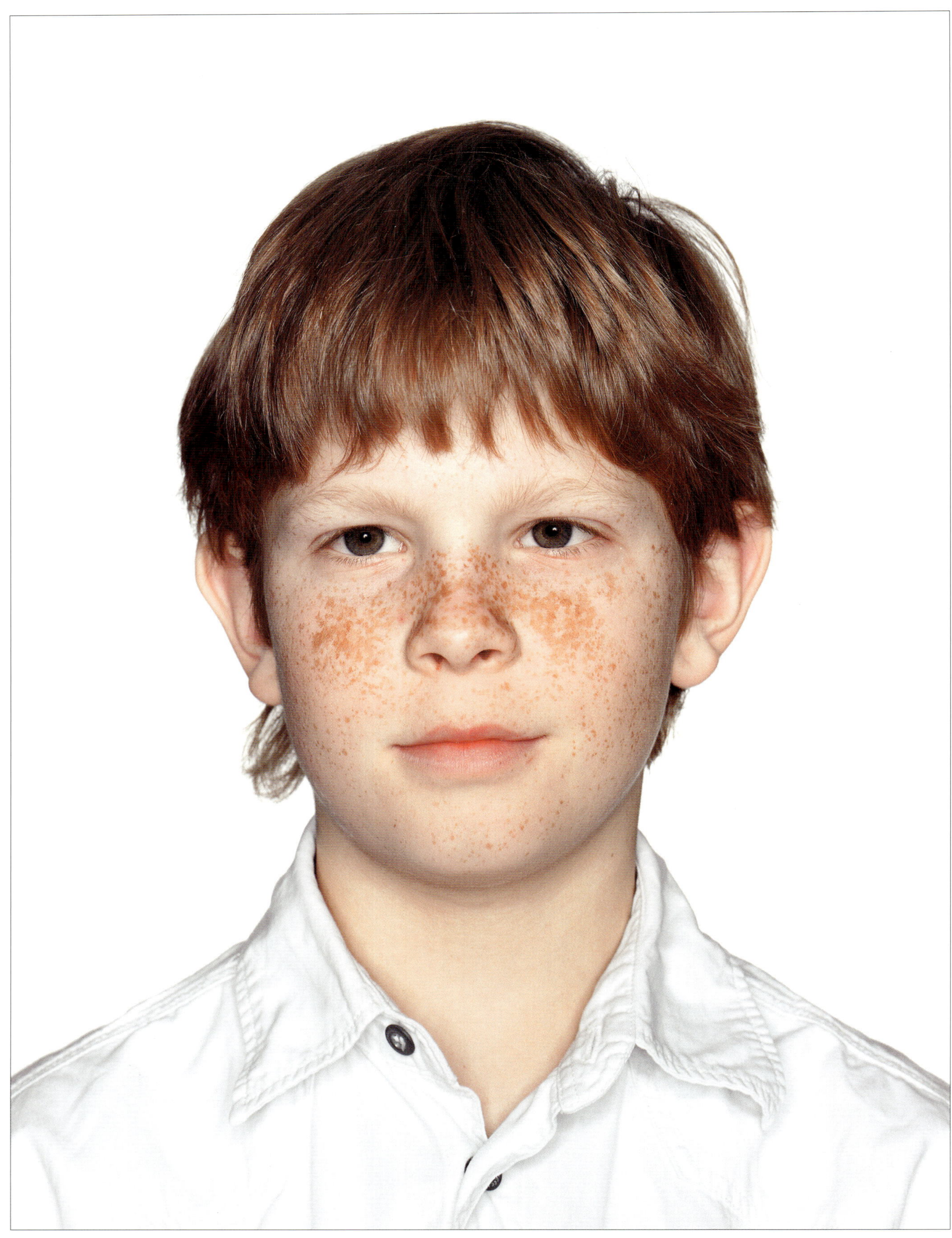

Maik Grieger

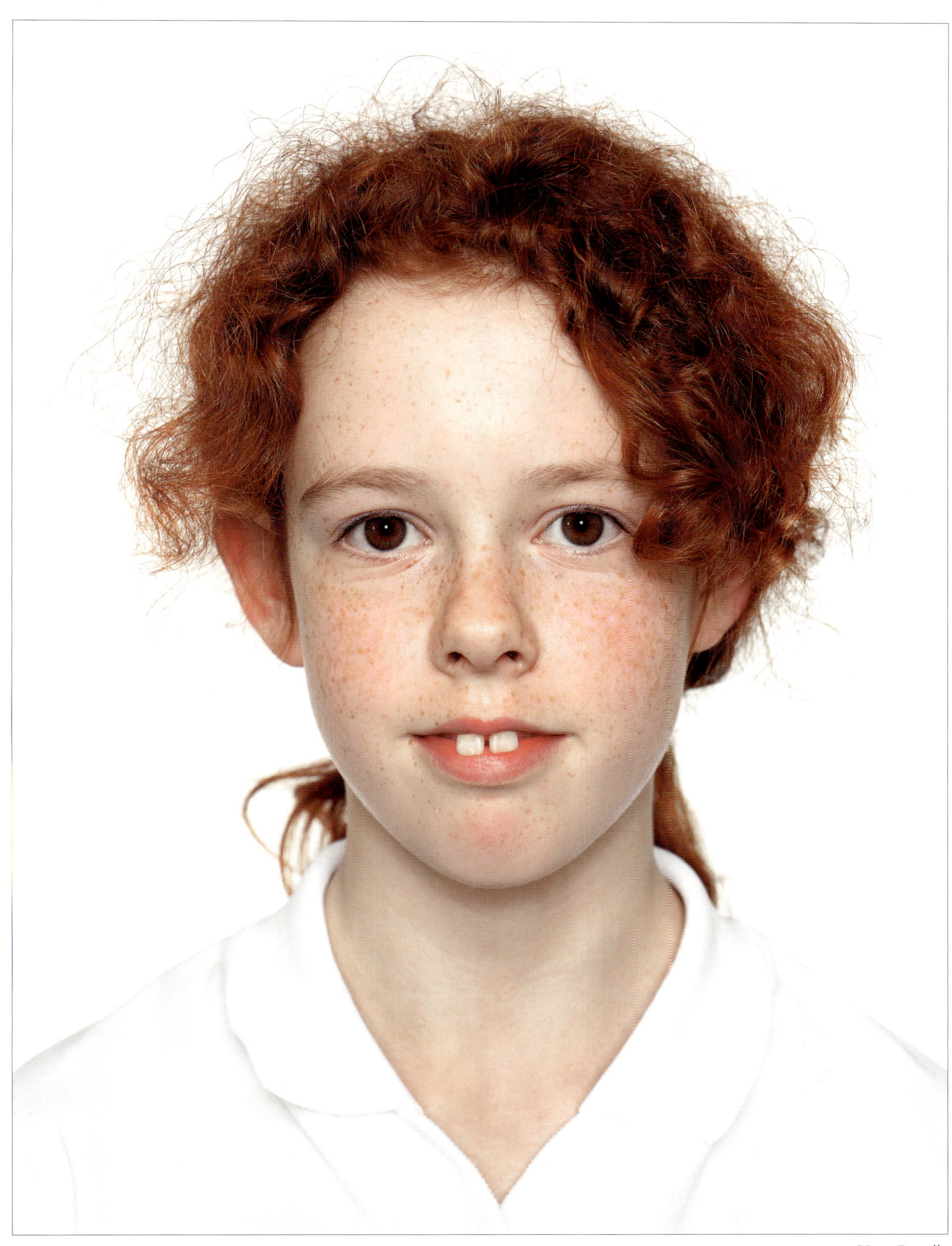

Mary Farrally

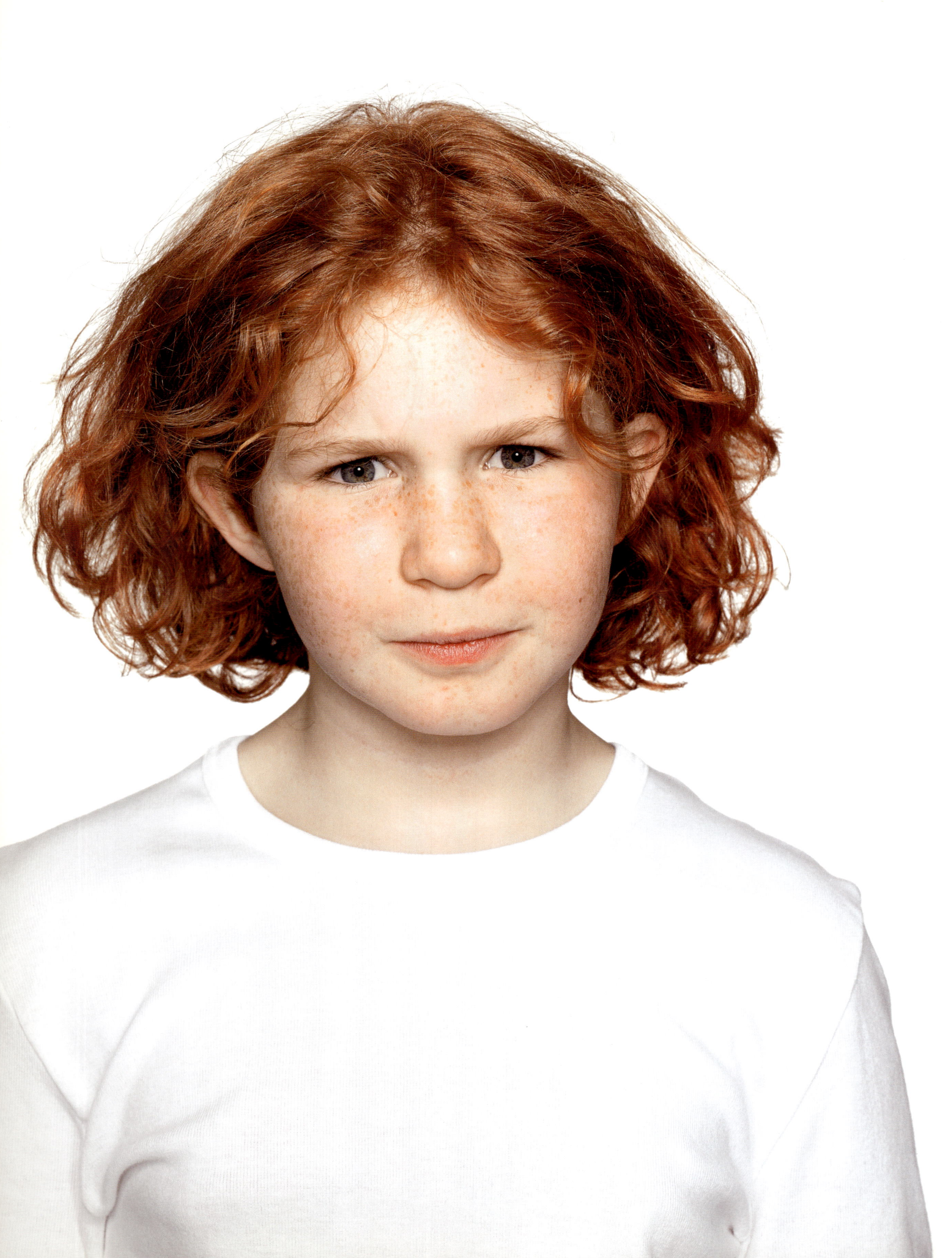

"It annoys me
when they call me 'ketchup-bottle.'
I like my hair."

"Red hair means
that I stand out more in a crowd,
which can make it difficult
when I'm trying
to be inconspicuous!"

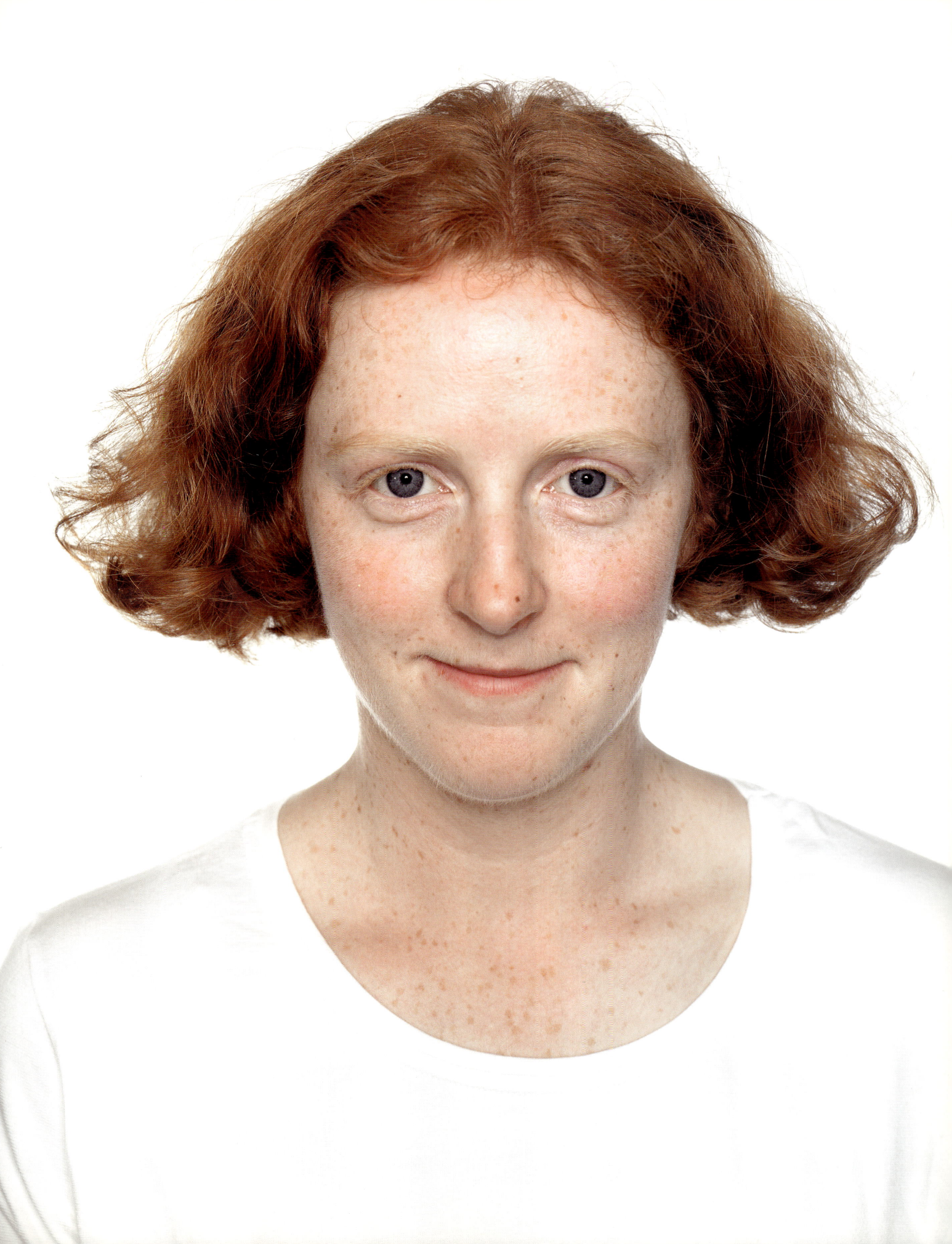

"My teacher calls me
Elisa Dolittle."

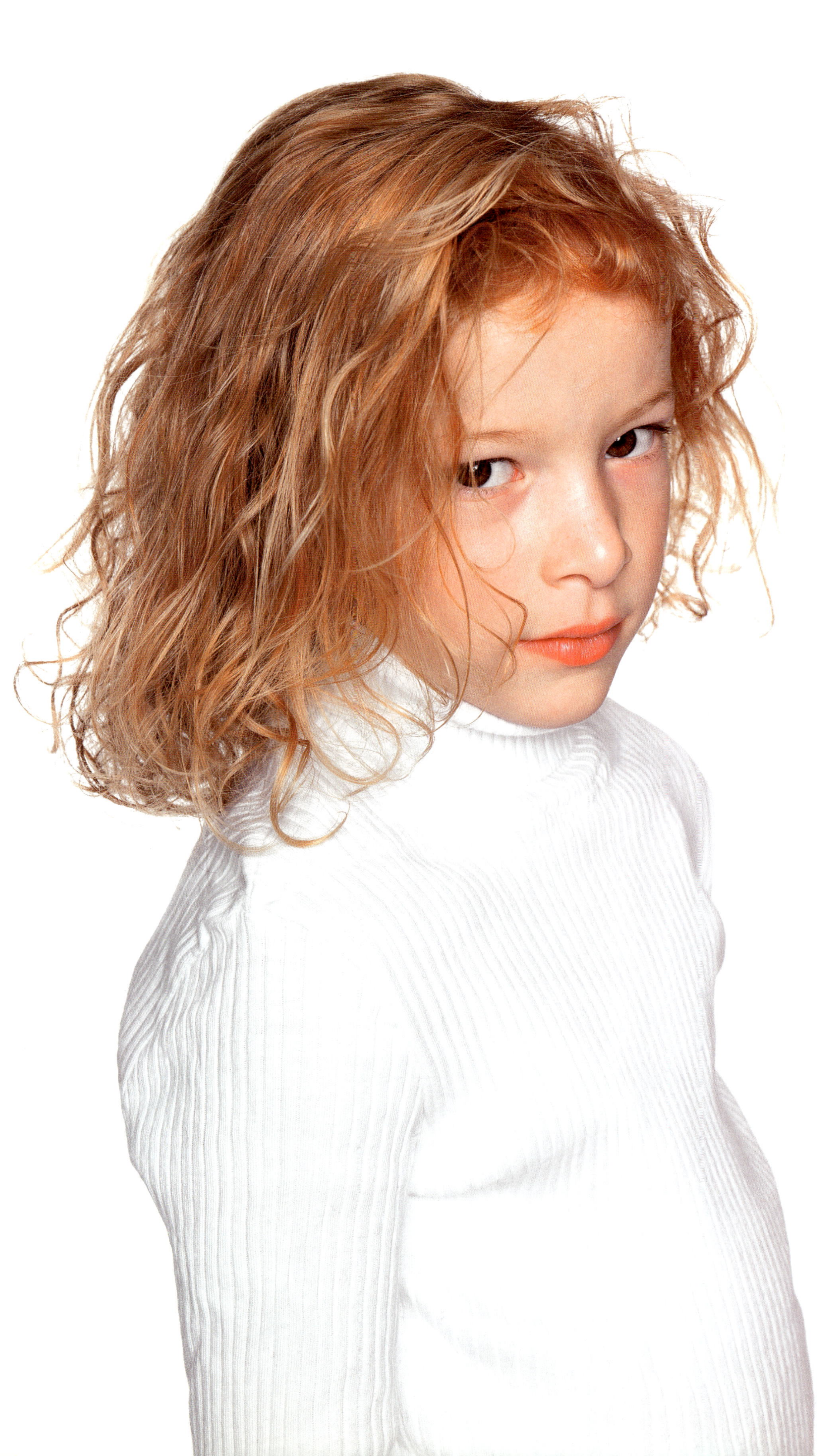

"I like the red hair
on my arms and legs—
I don't even know why!"

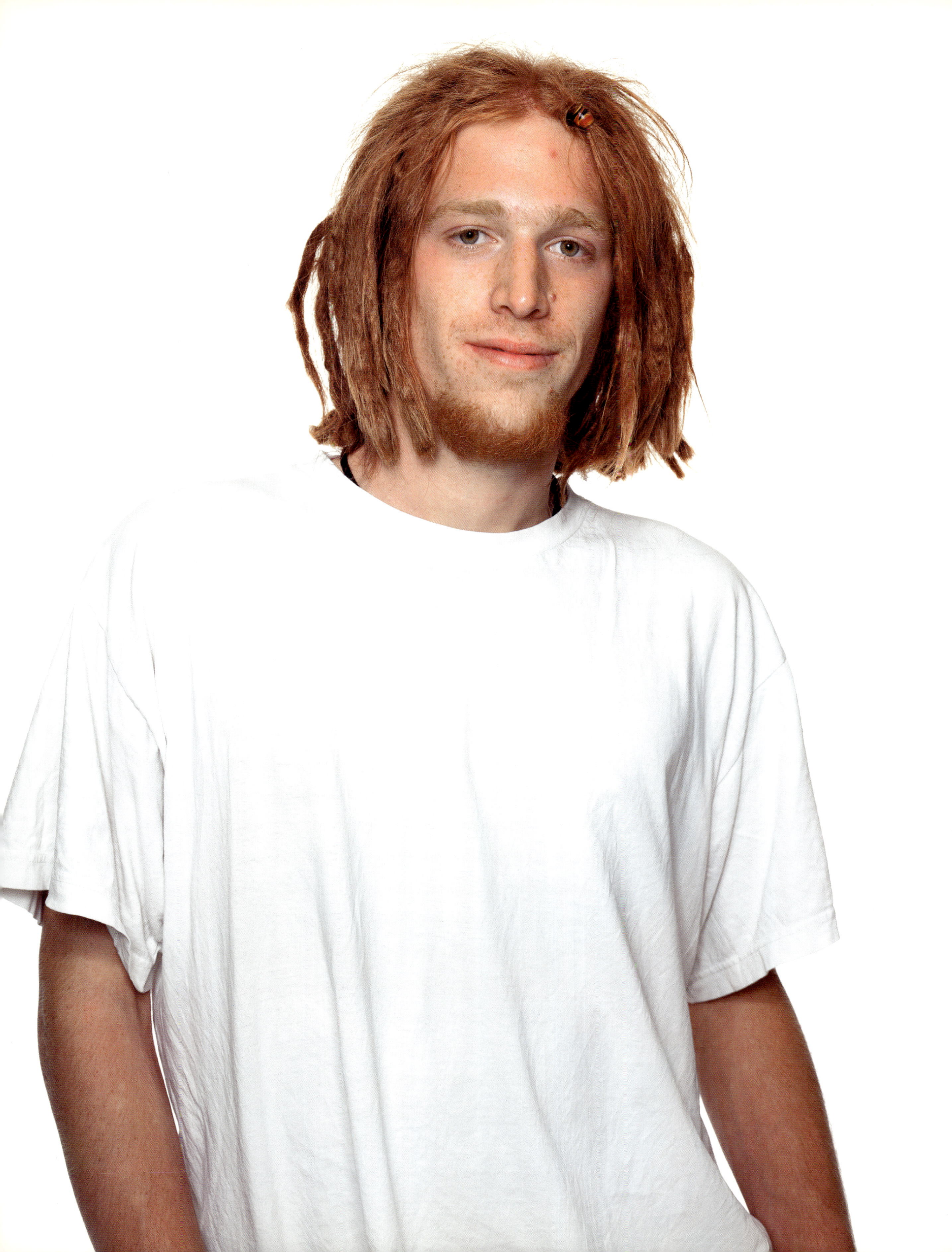

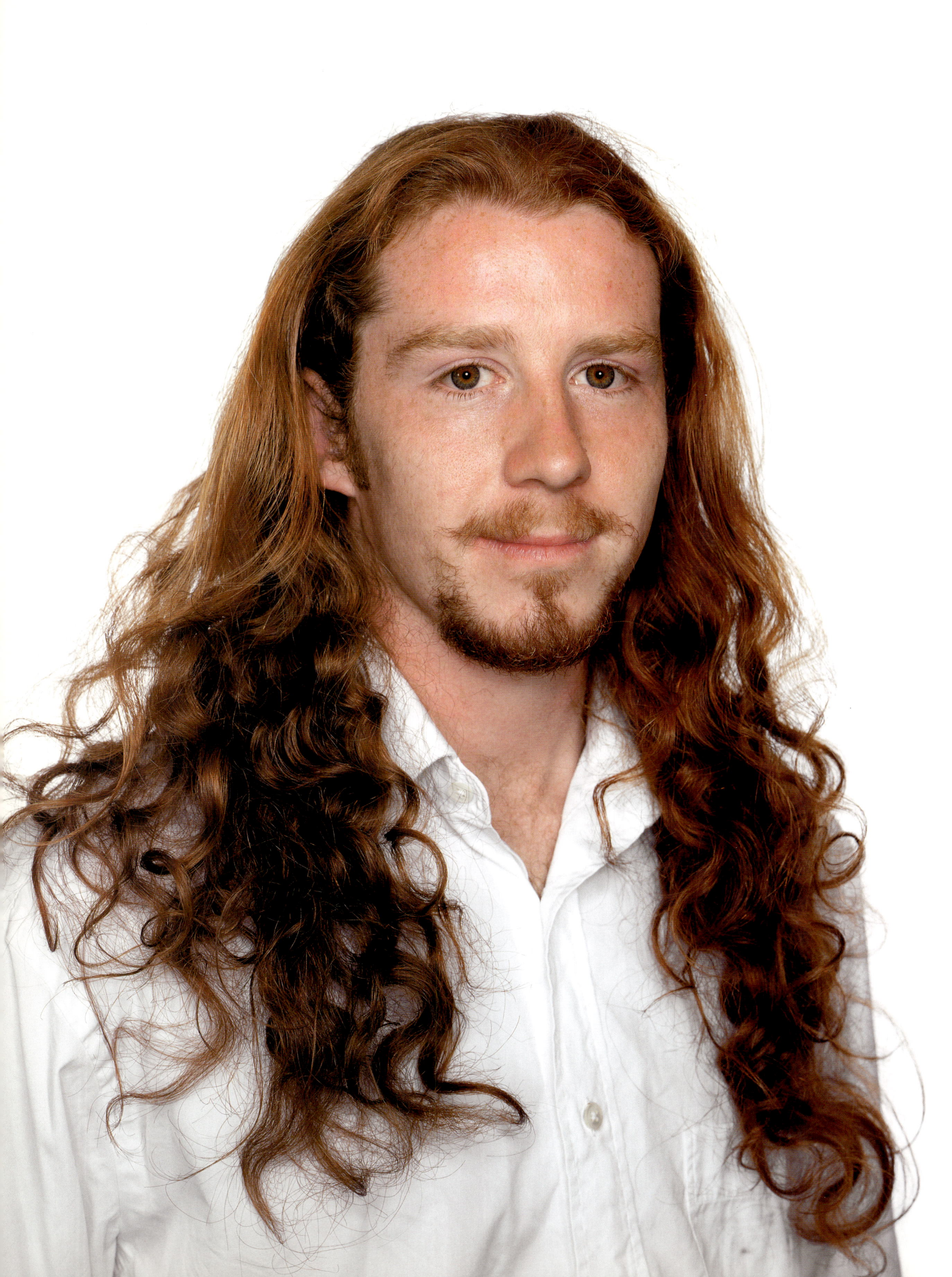

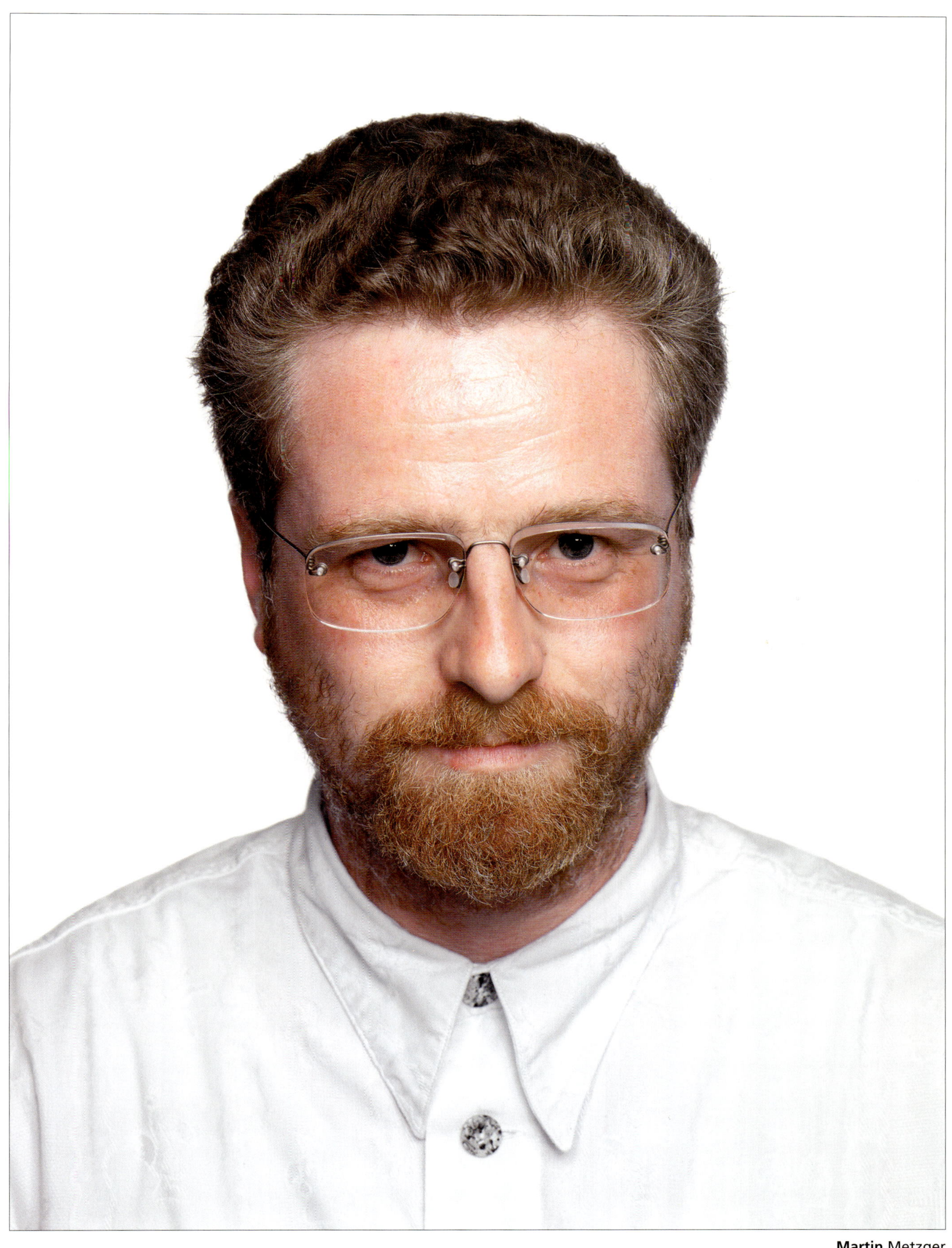

Martin Metzger

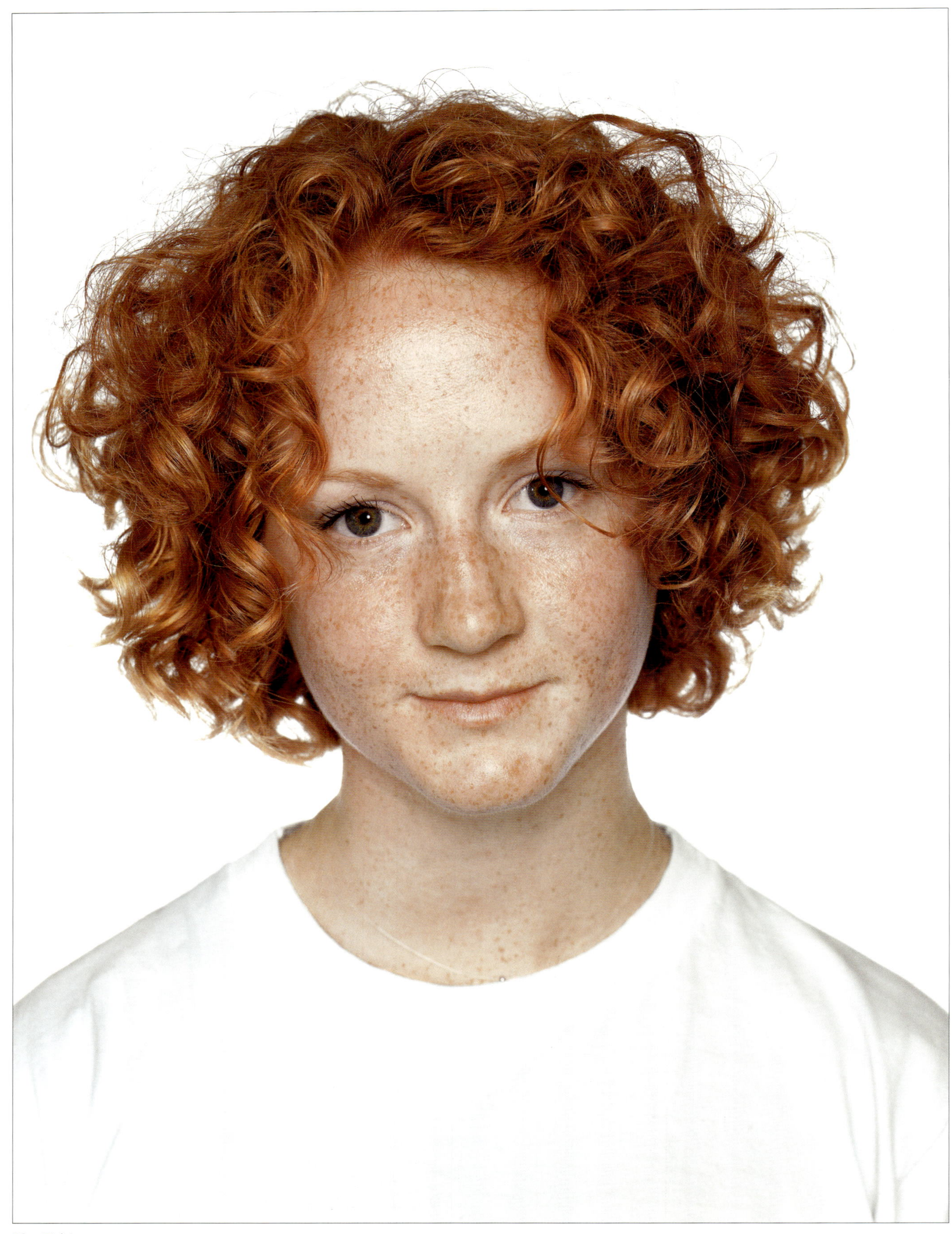

Rita Tobin

"I'm happy
that my hair can pull people
from their realities
and wake them
to visual pleasure."

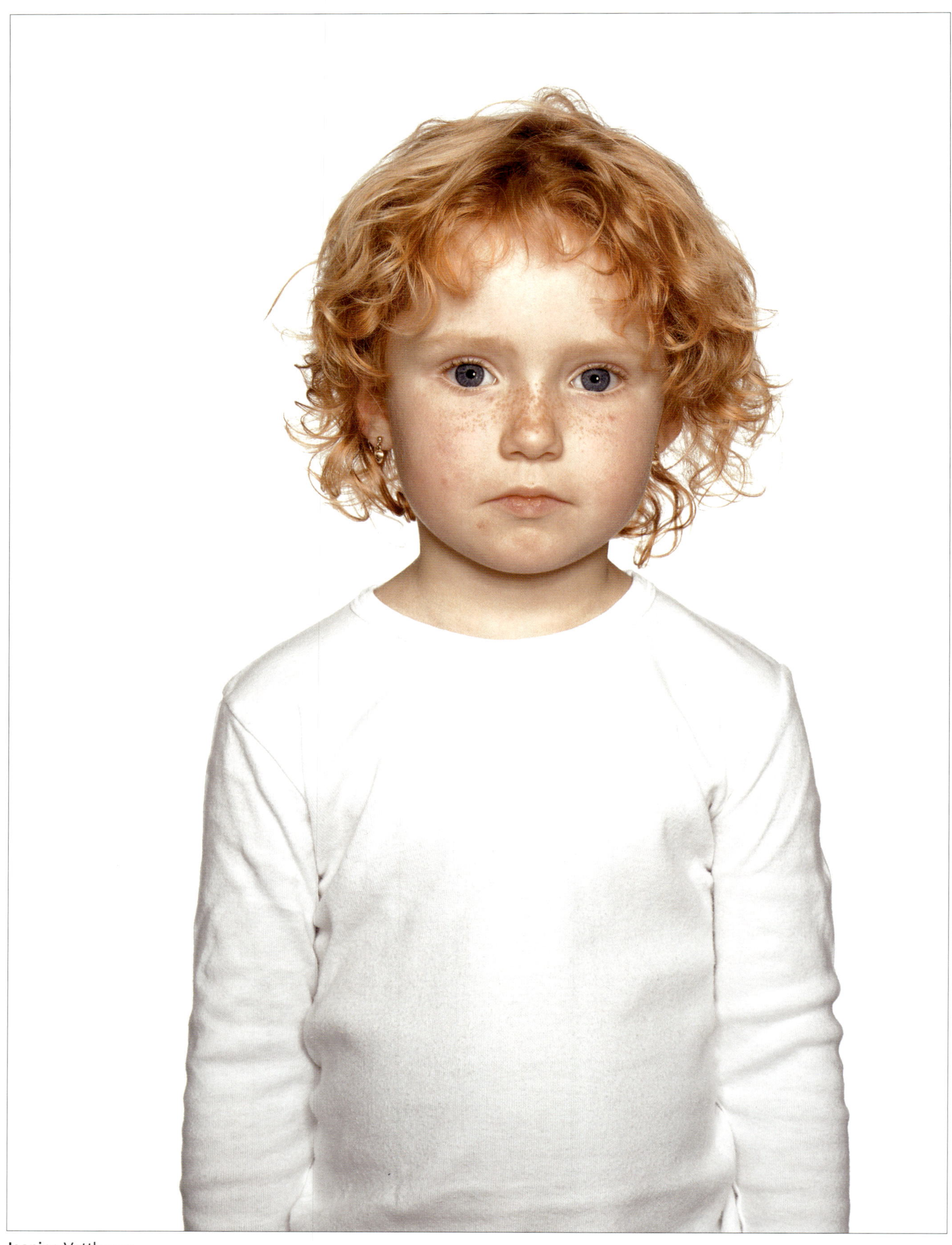

Jeanine Vattheuer

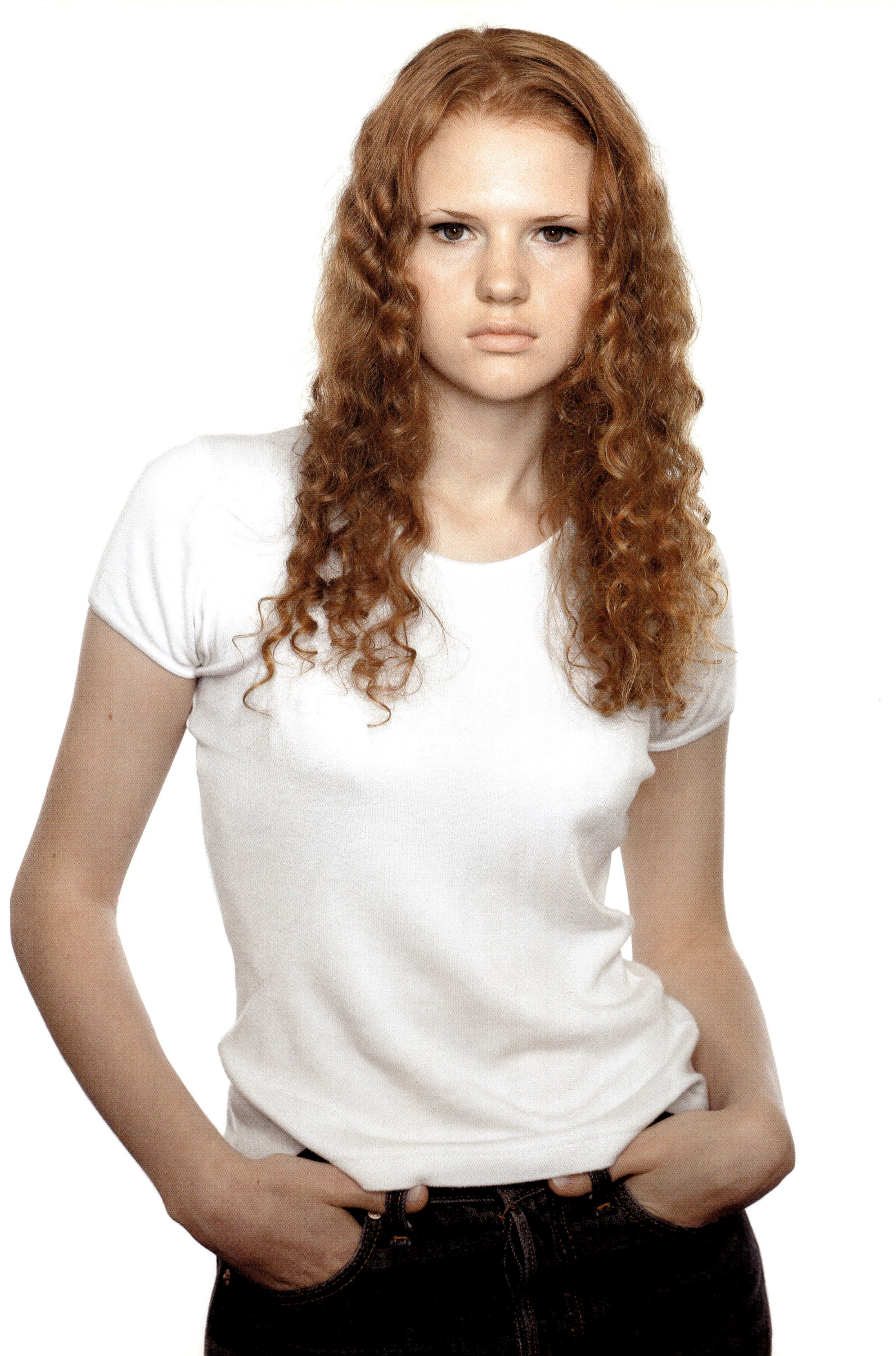

"For me, red means power,
force and eroticism."

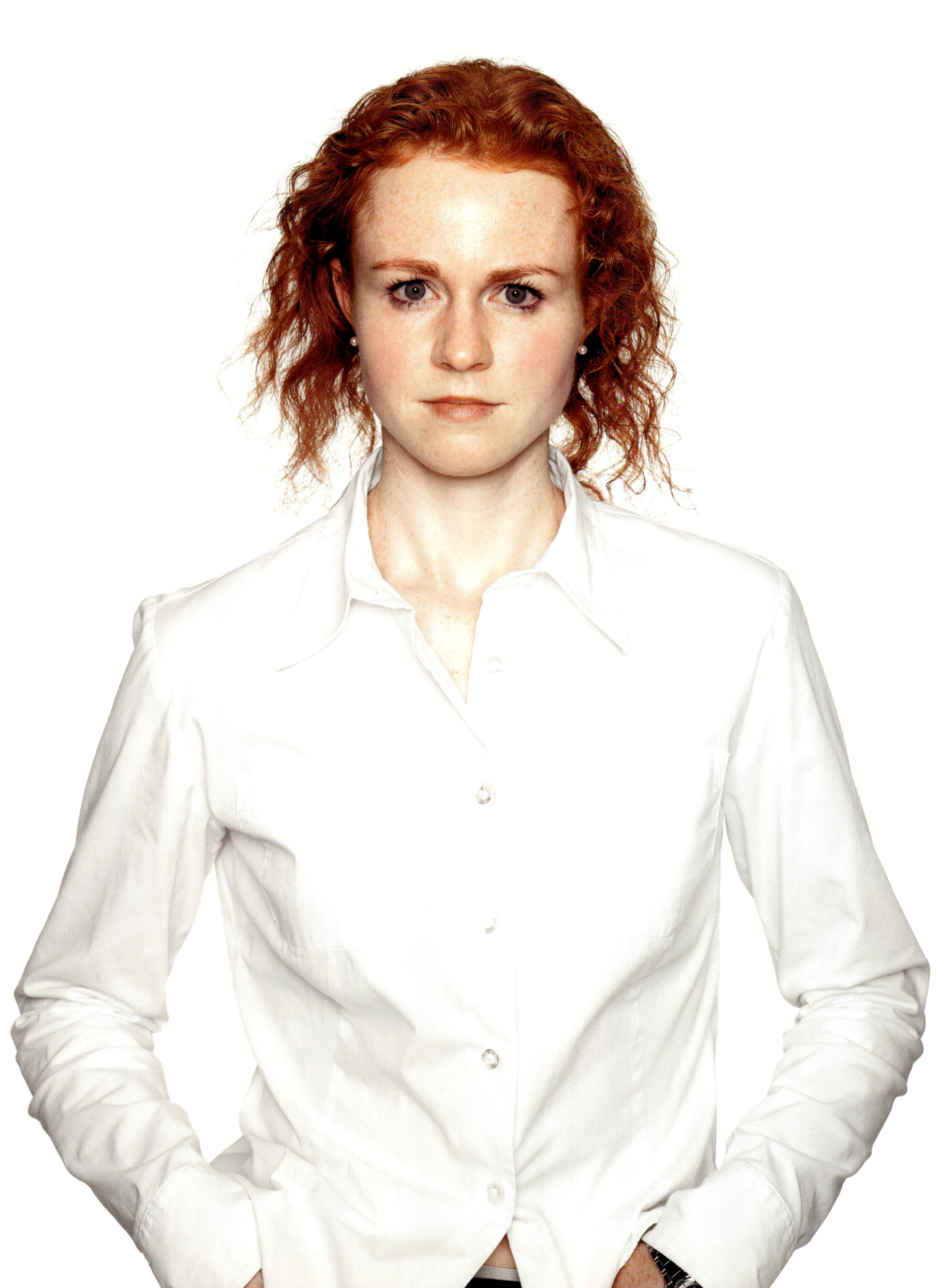

"My skin has a lot of freckles.
People say they are a sign of beauty."

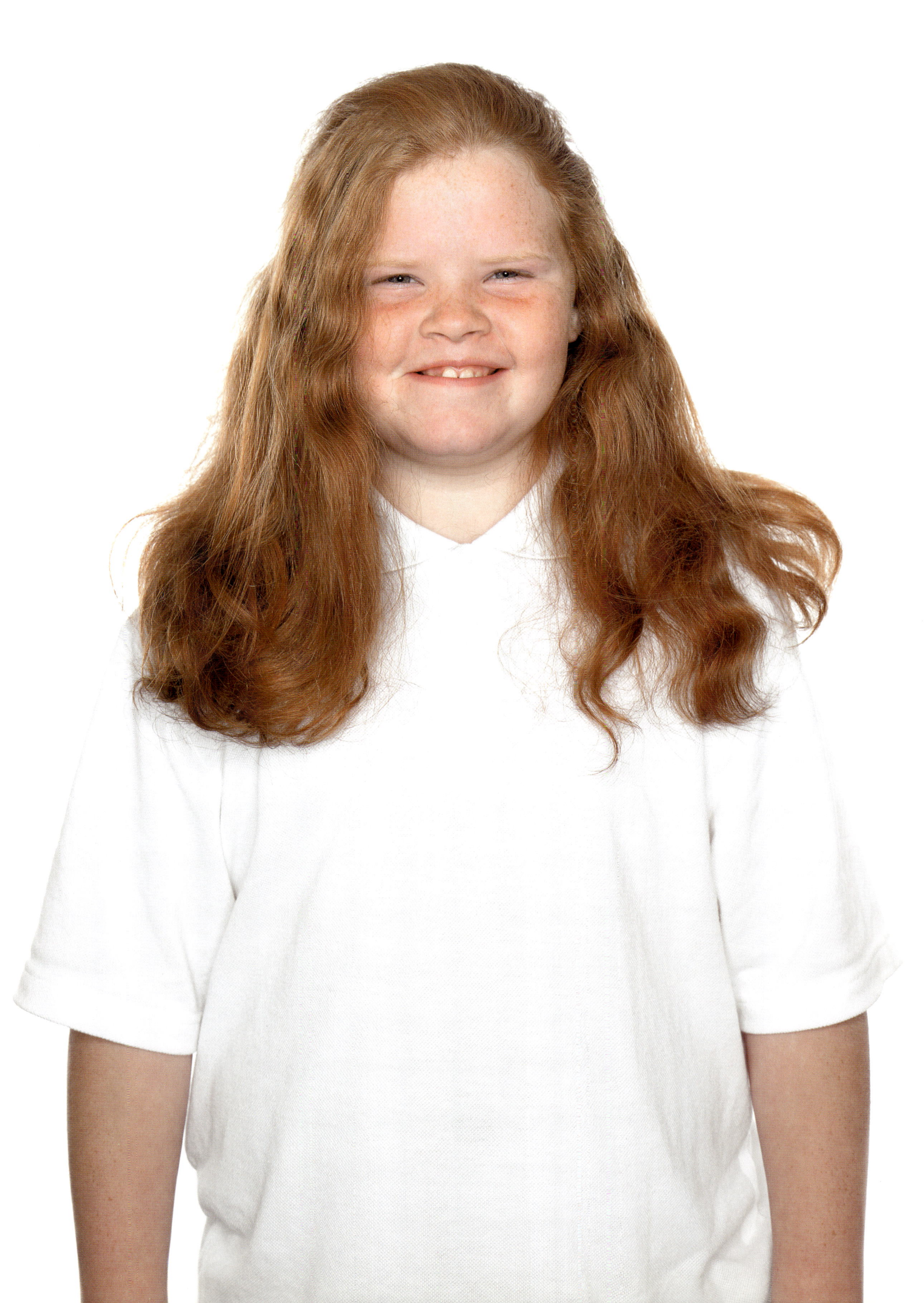

"People always seem
to notice red hair
more than any other color hair.
This makes me feel important."

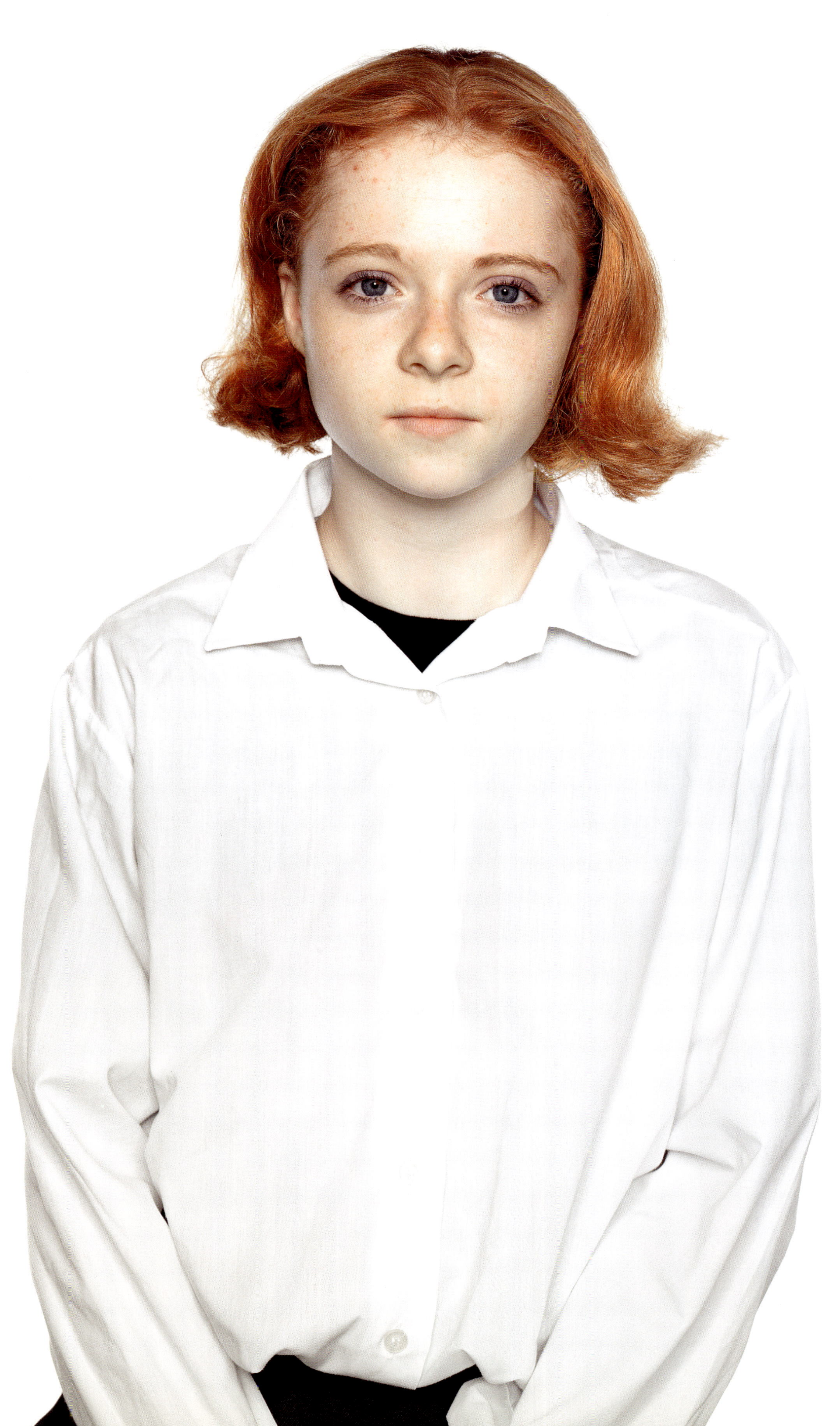

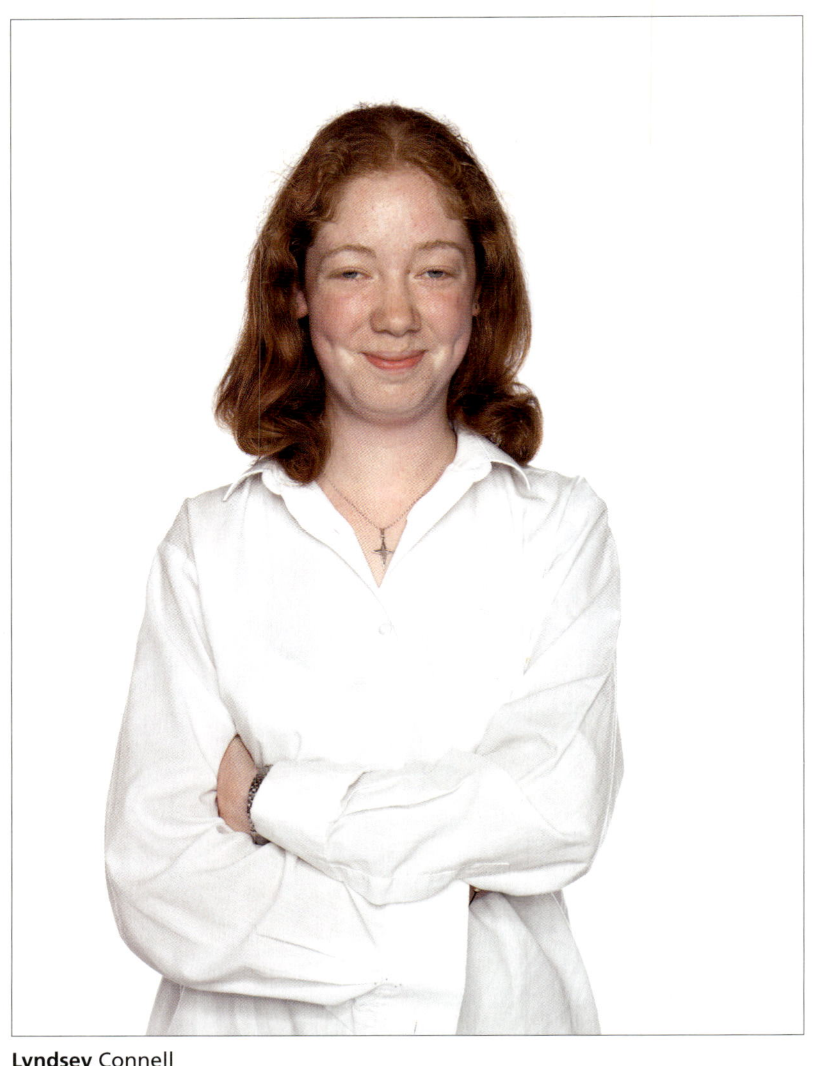

Lyndsey Connell

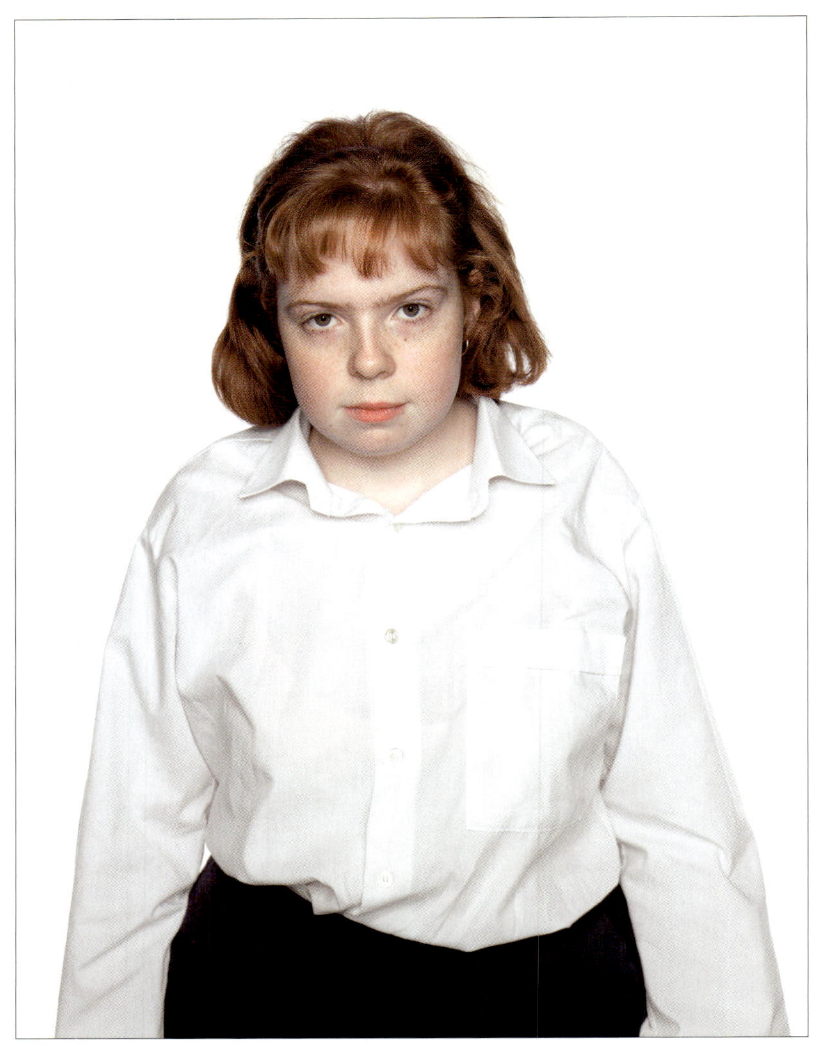

Emma O'Donnell

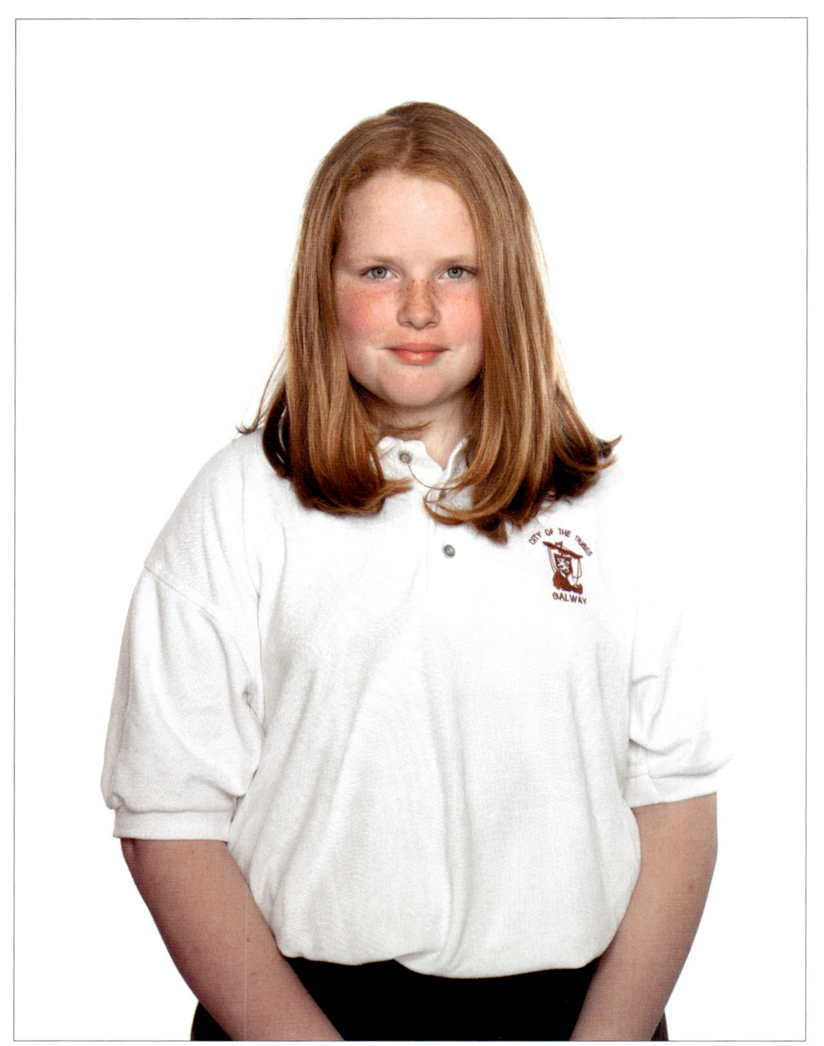

Erin Kelly

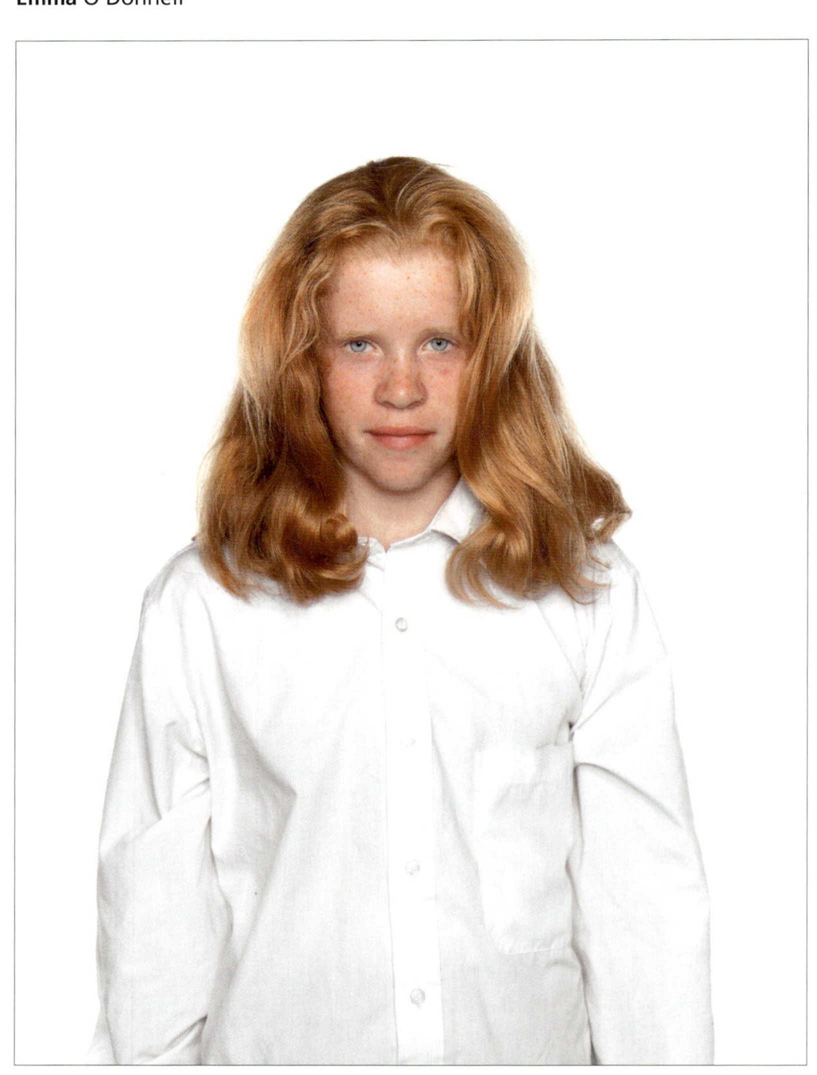

Catherine McDonagh

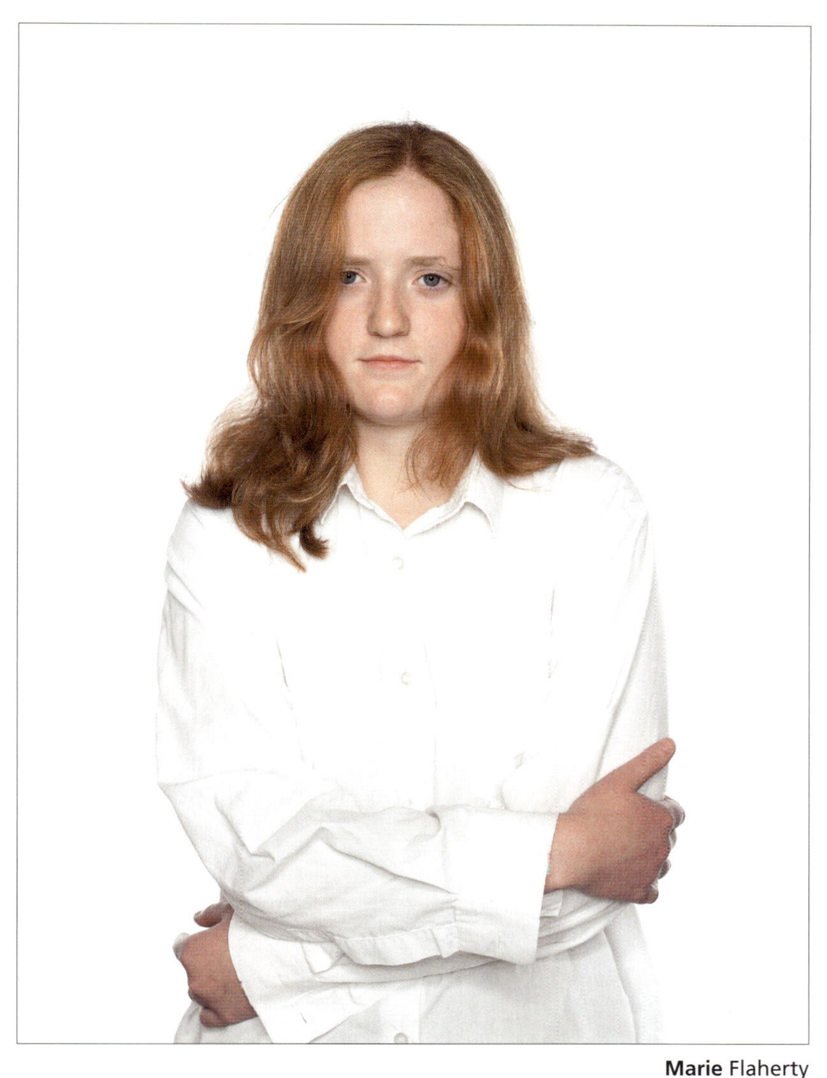

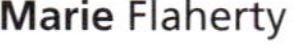

Marie Flaherty

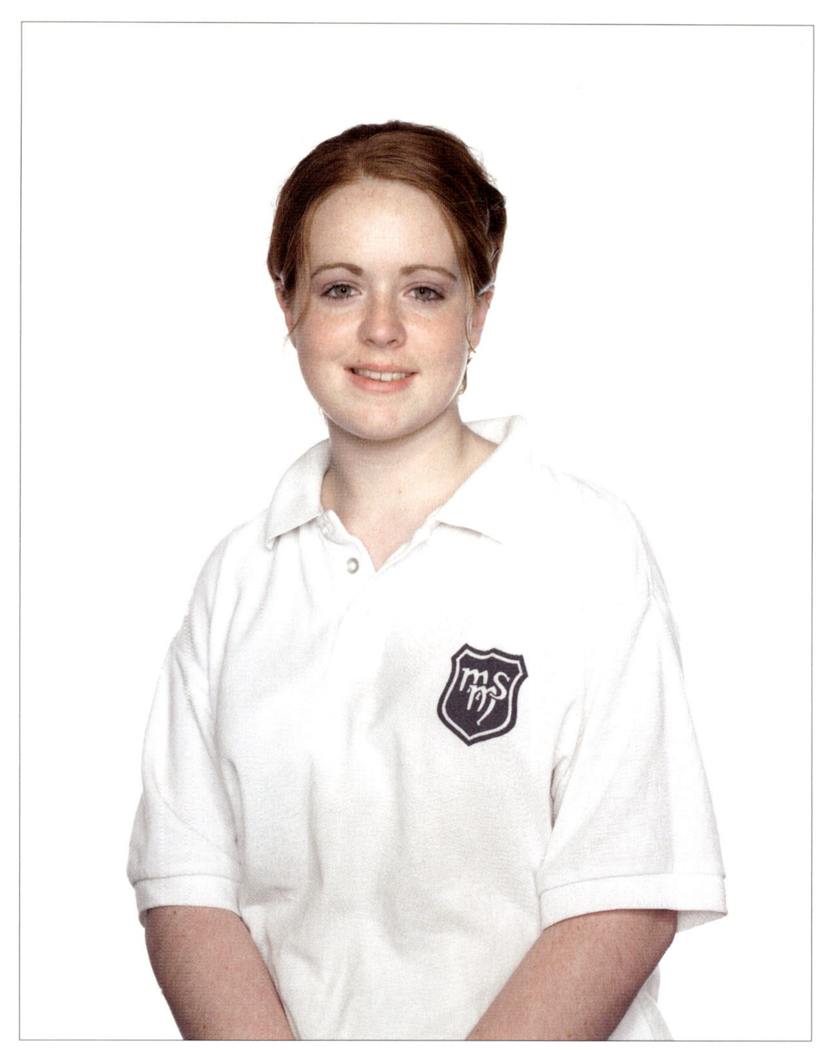

Arlene Glynn

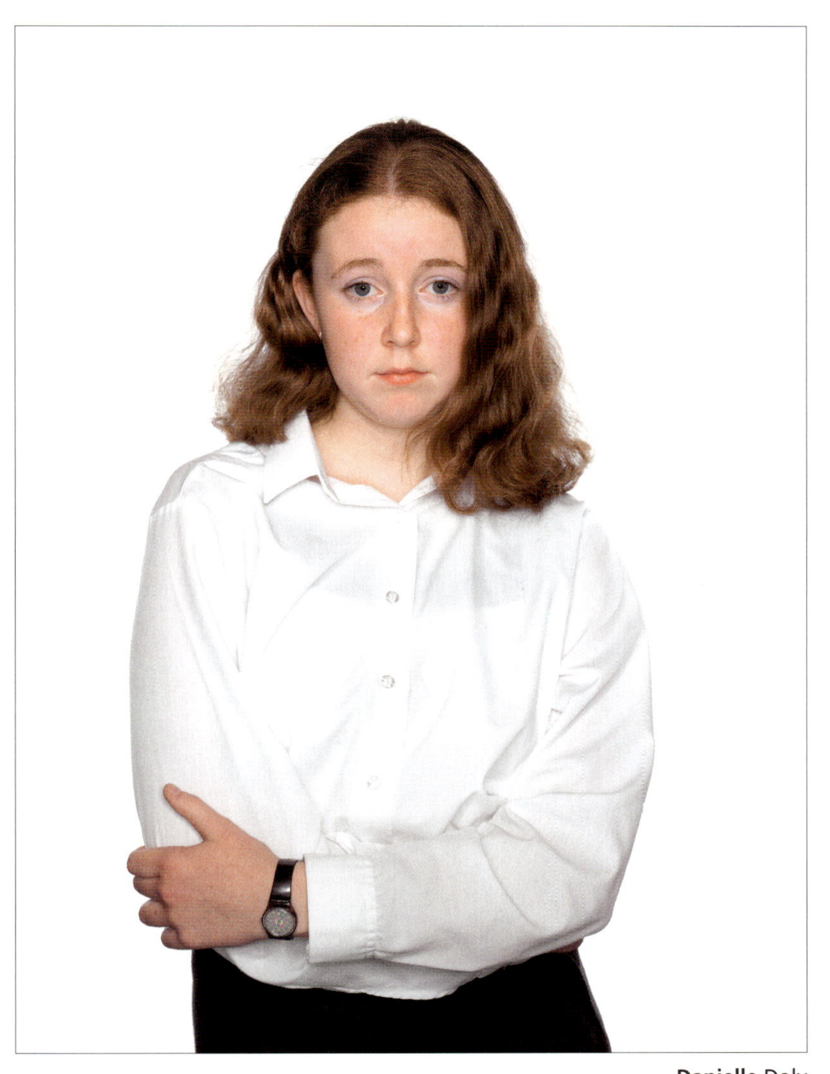

Danielle Daly

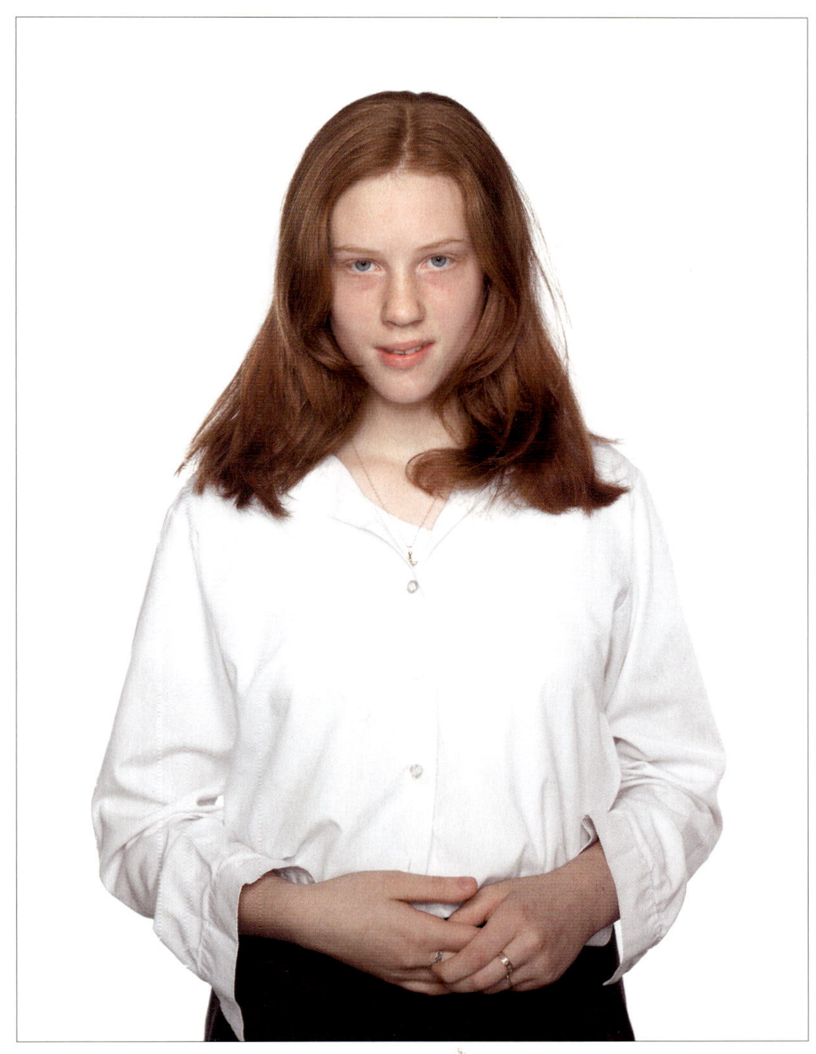

Sinéad McErlain

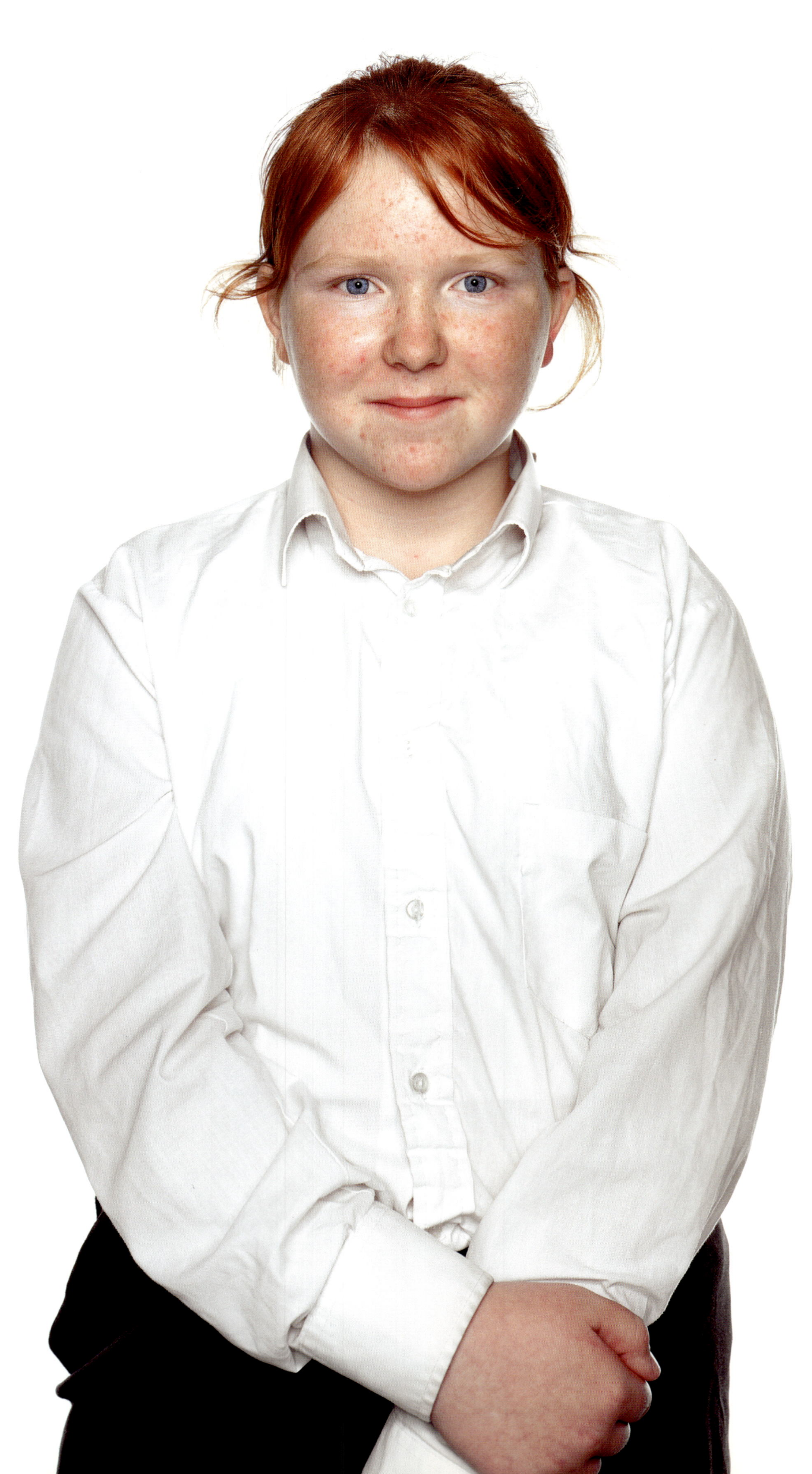

"I think having red hair means
I have a fiery personality."

"Girls liked me,
boys did not.
That's the story of my life!"

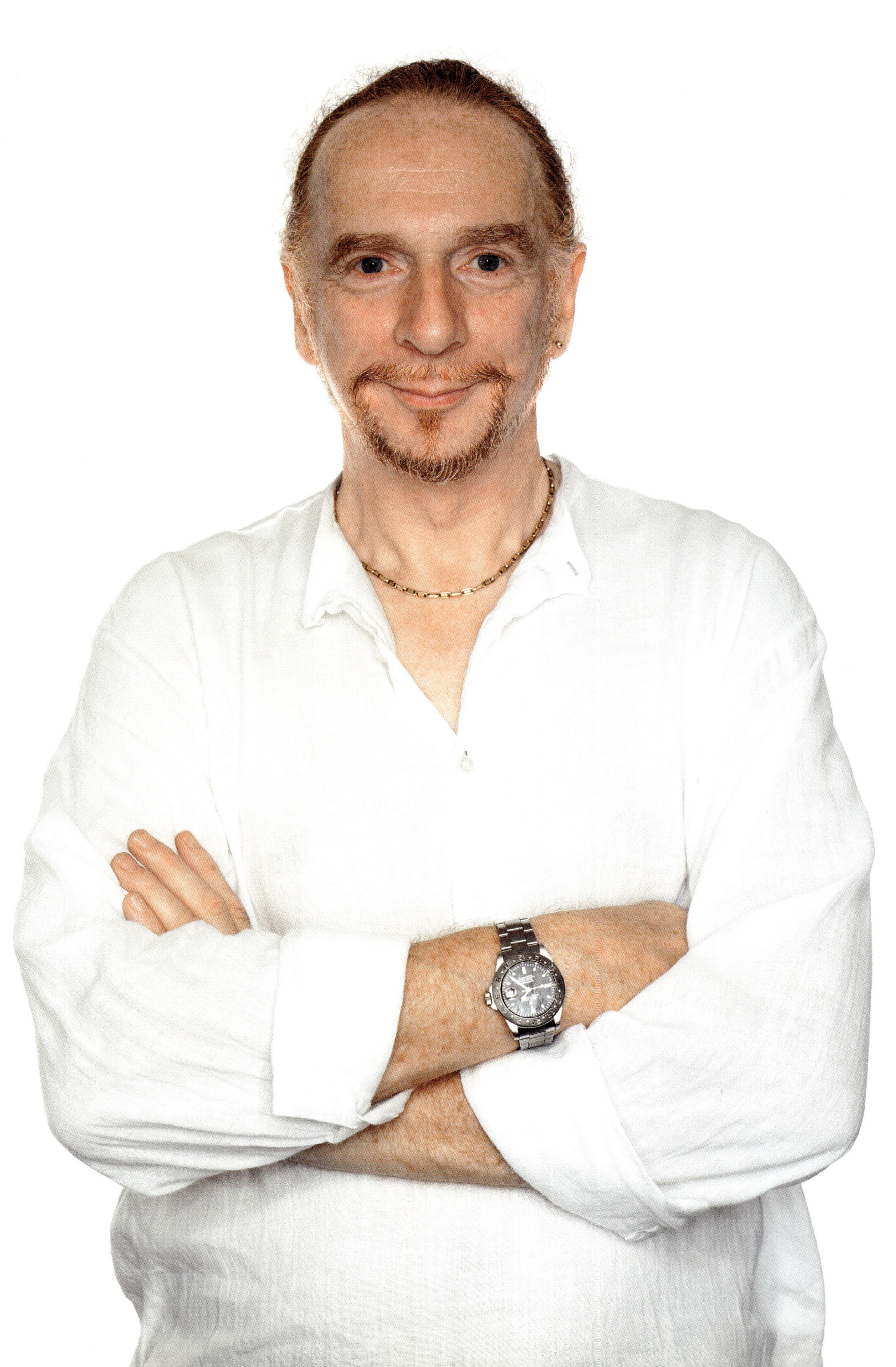

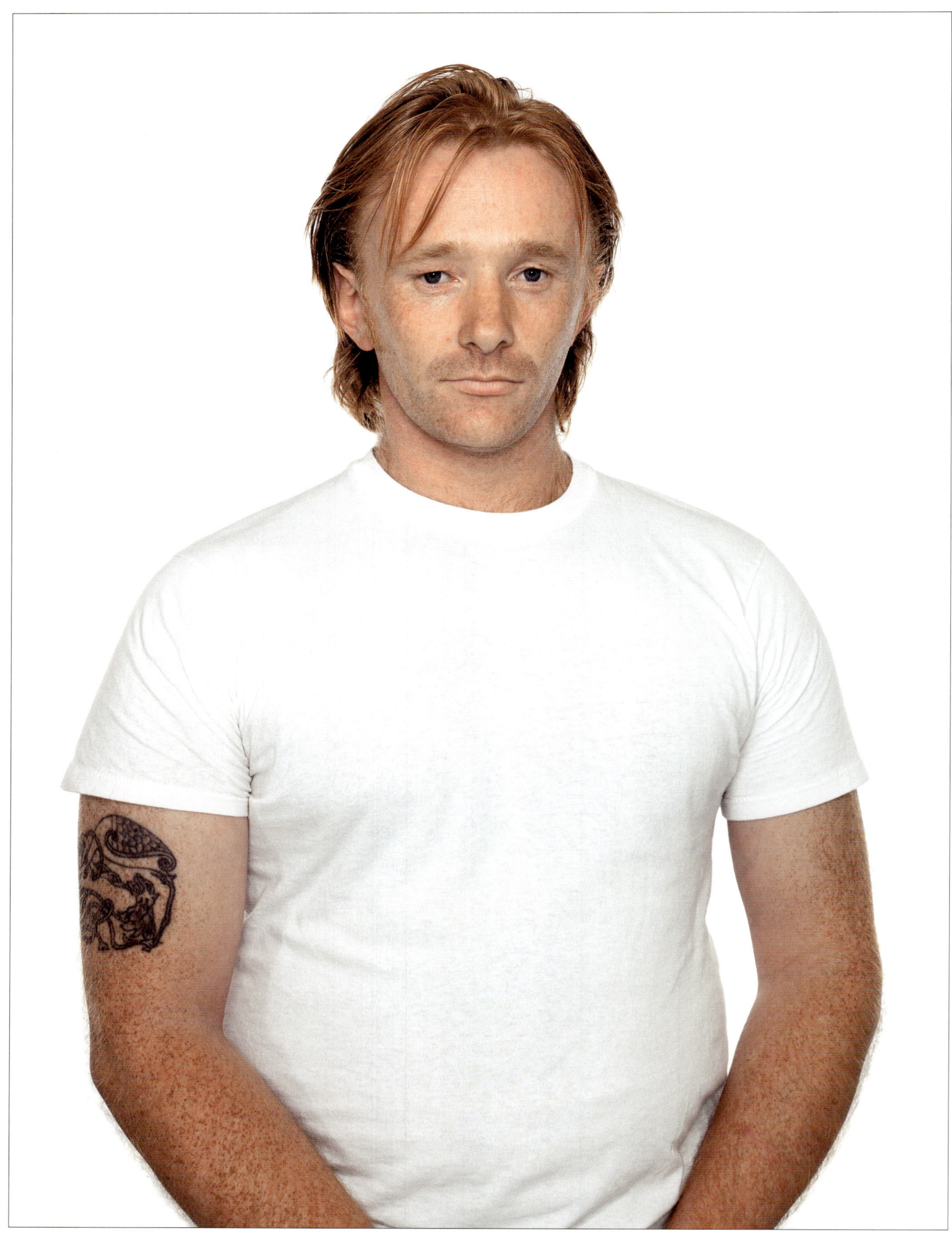

Nicholas Flood

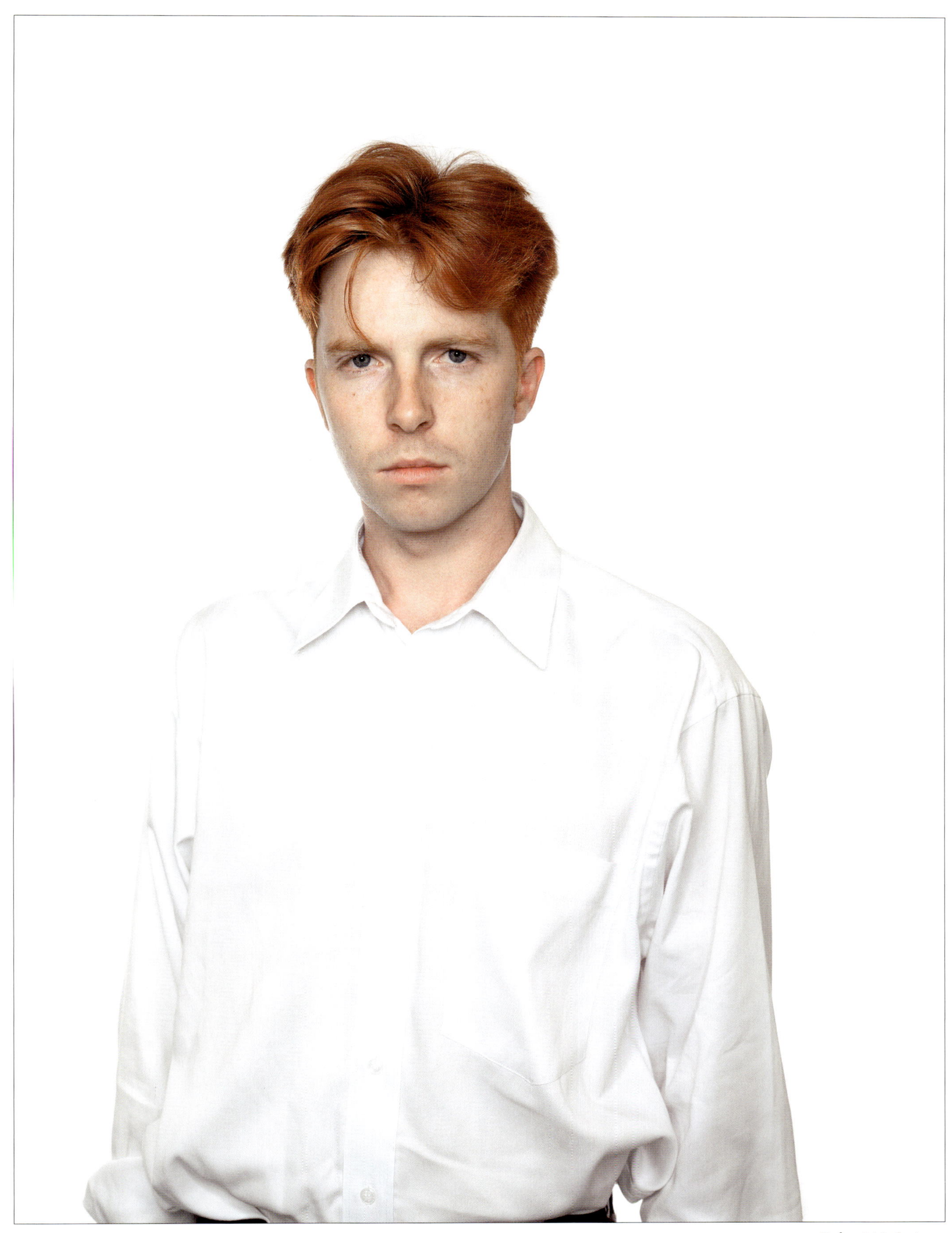

Robert McCartney

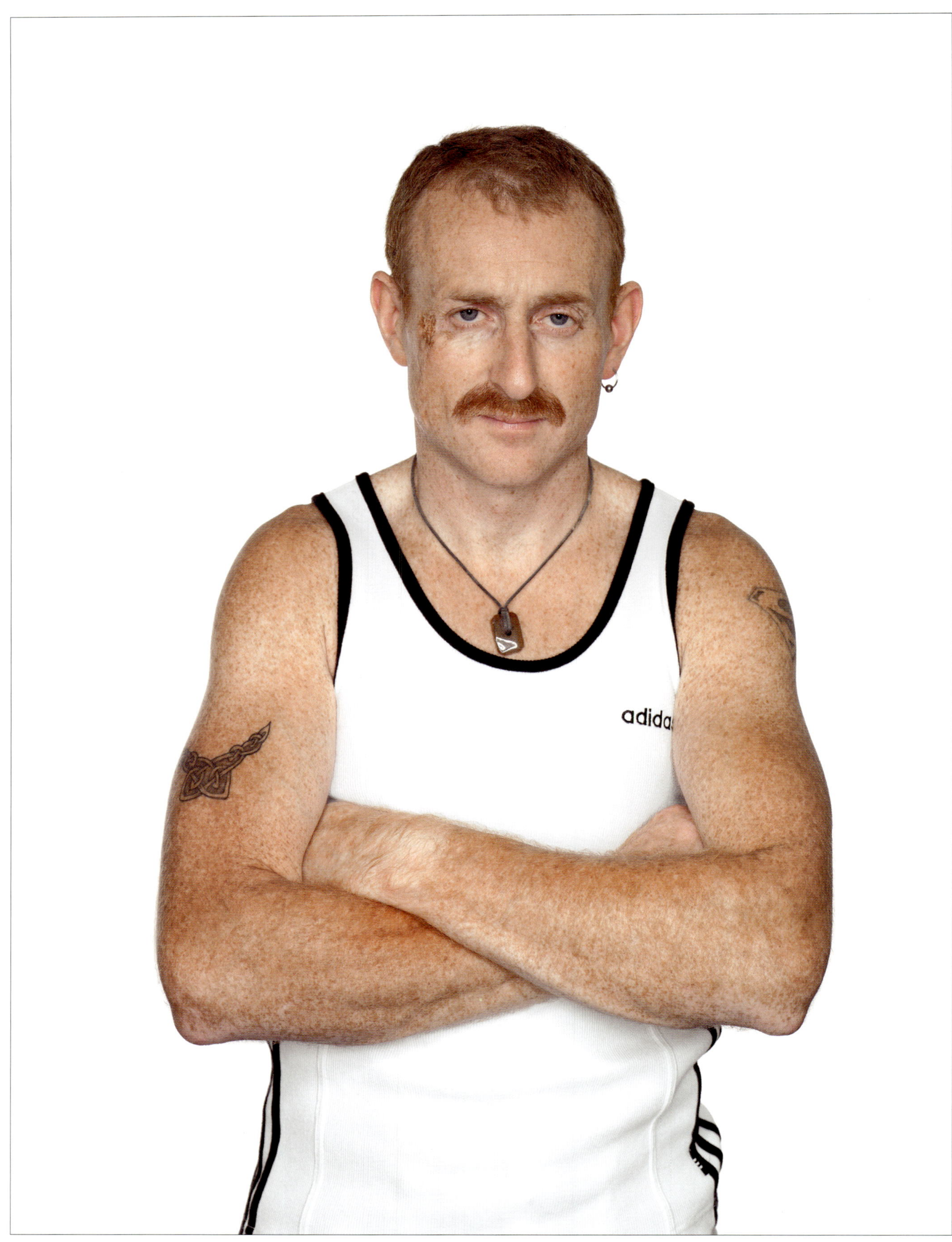

Richard Byrne

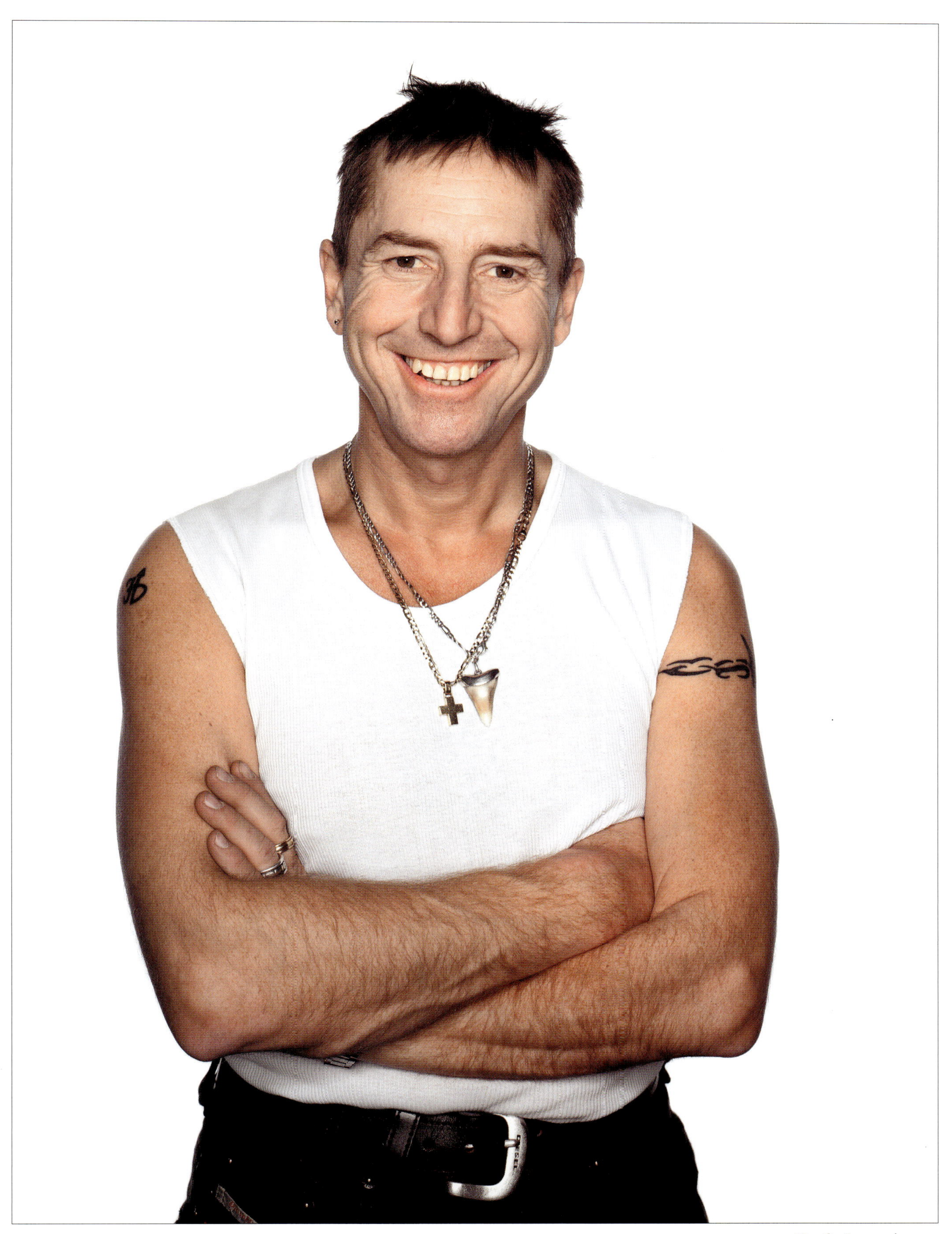

Martin Semmelrogge

"Having red hair
holds little significance
to who I am;
I mean, it's just a color,
right?"

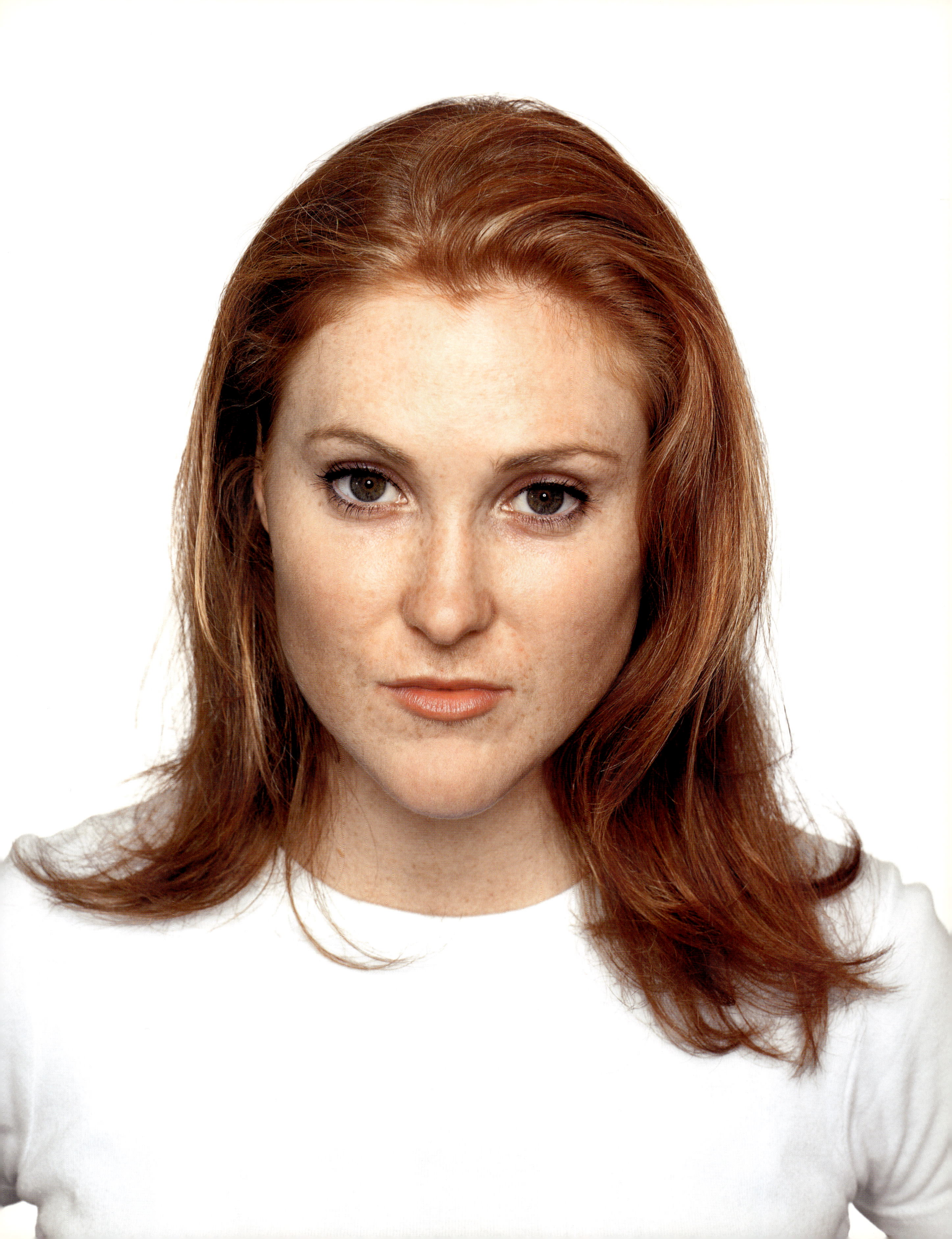

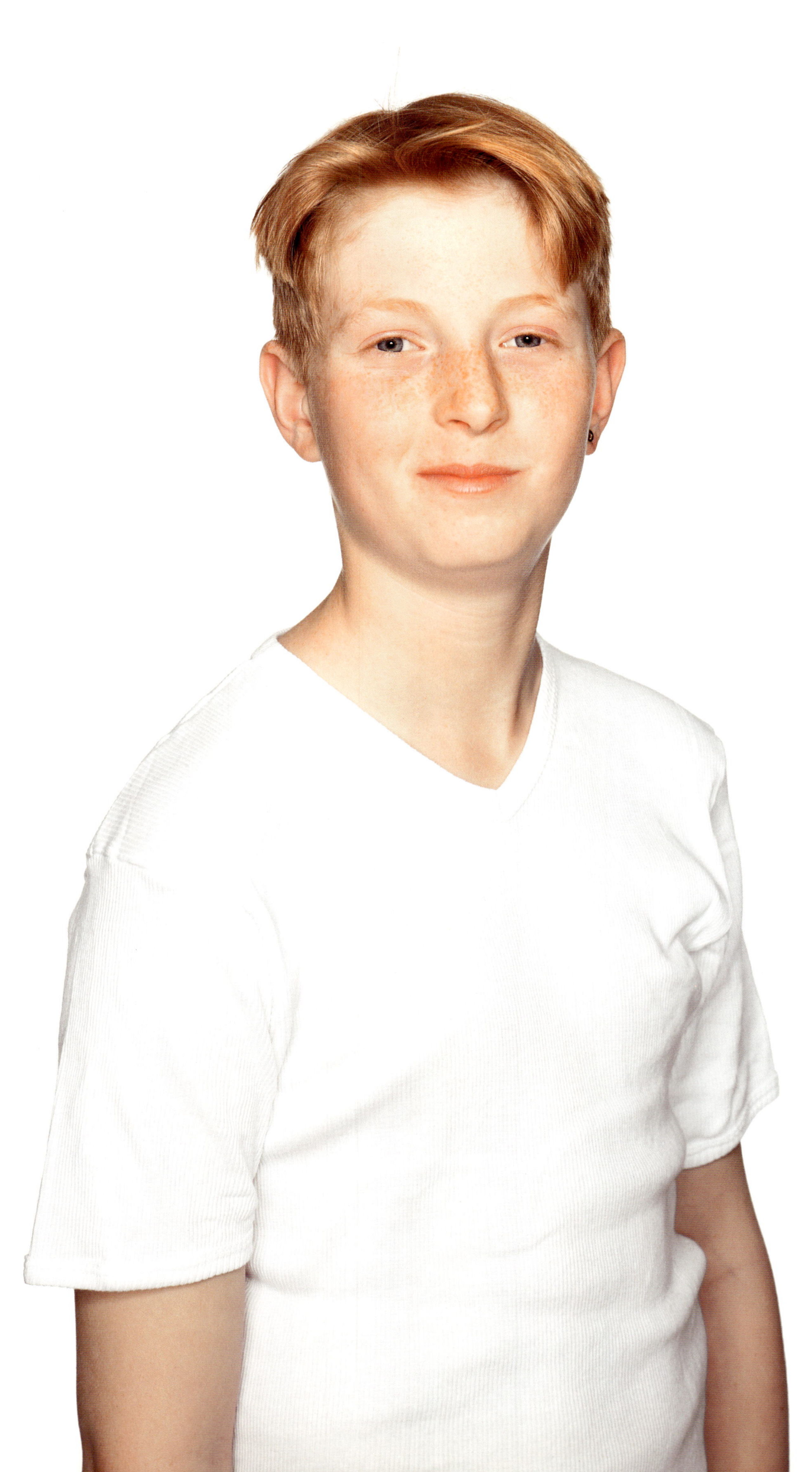

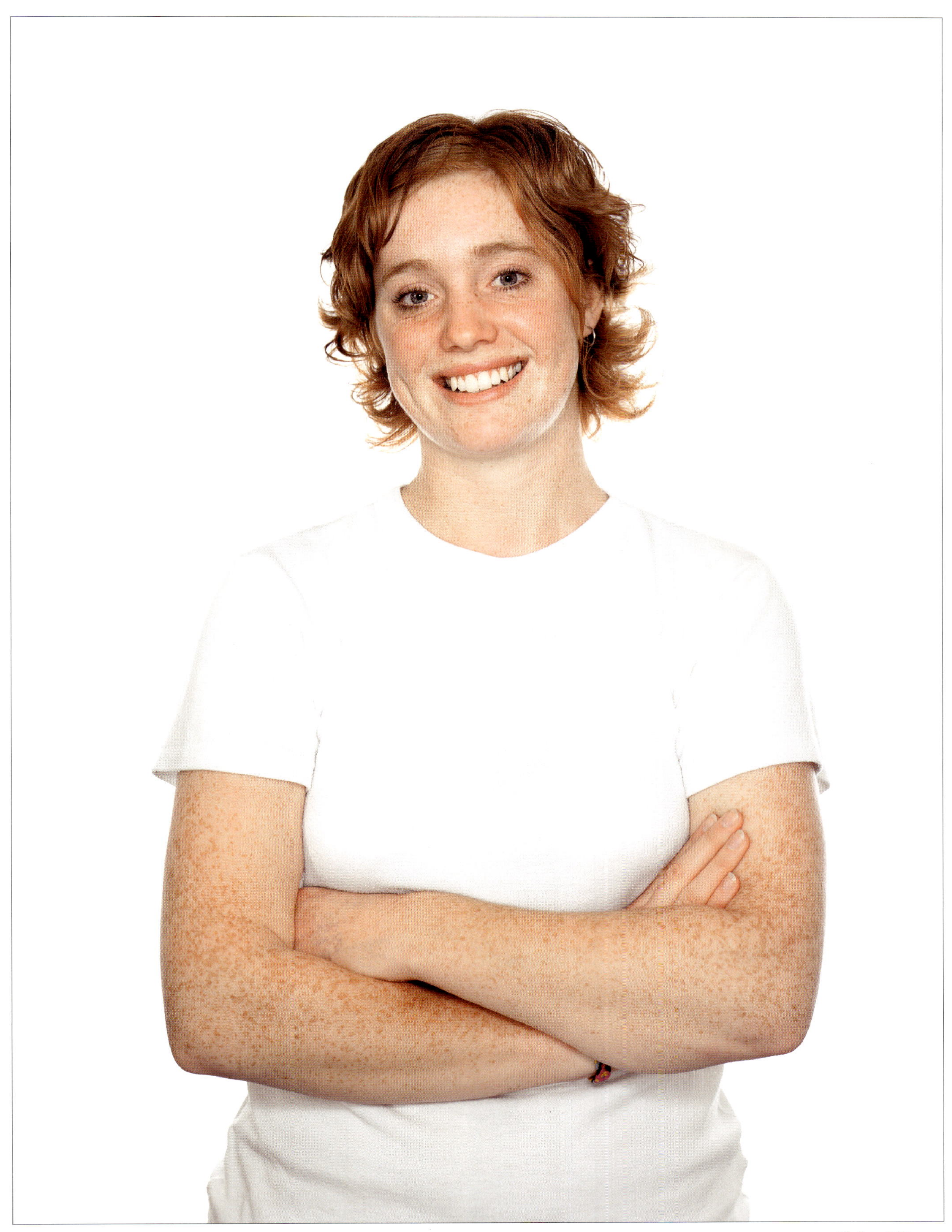

Elaine O'Dwyer

**"What I like about my hair
is that it glows.
What I don't like
is that it doesn't glow even more!"**

Sara-Patricia Zeh

Marc-Oliver & **Sara-Patricia** Zeh, father and daughter

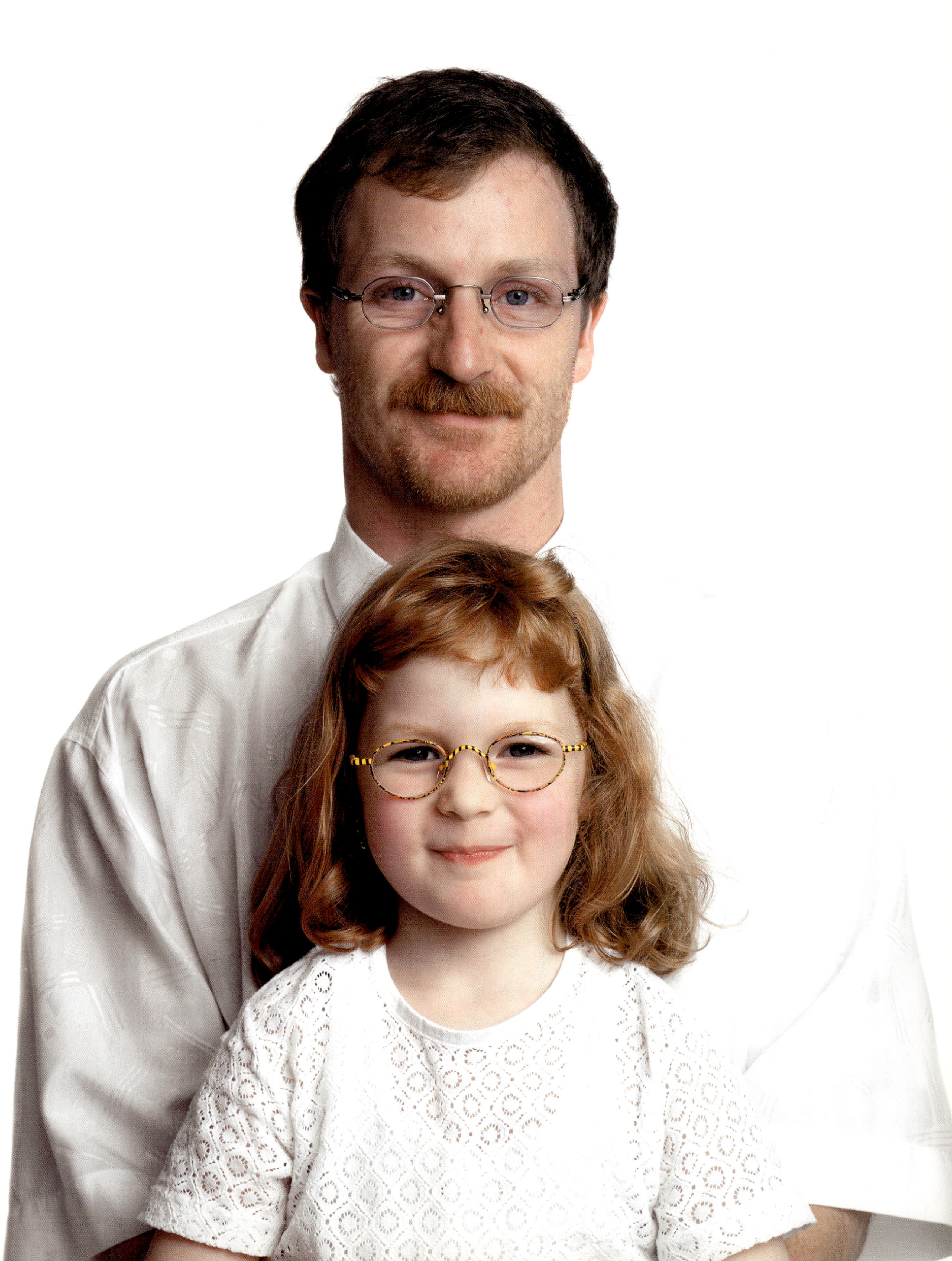

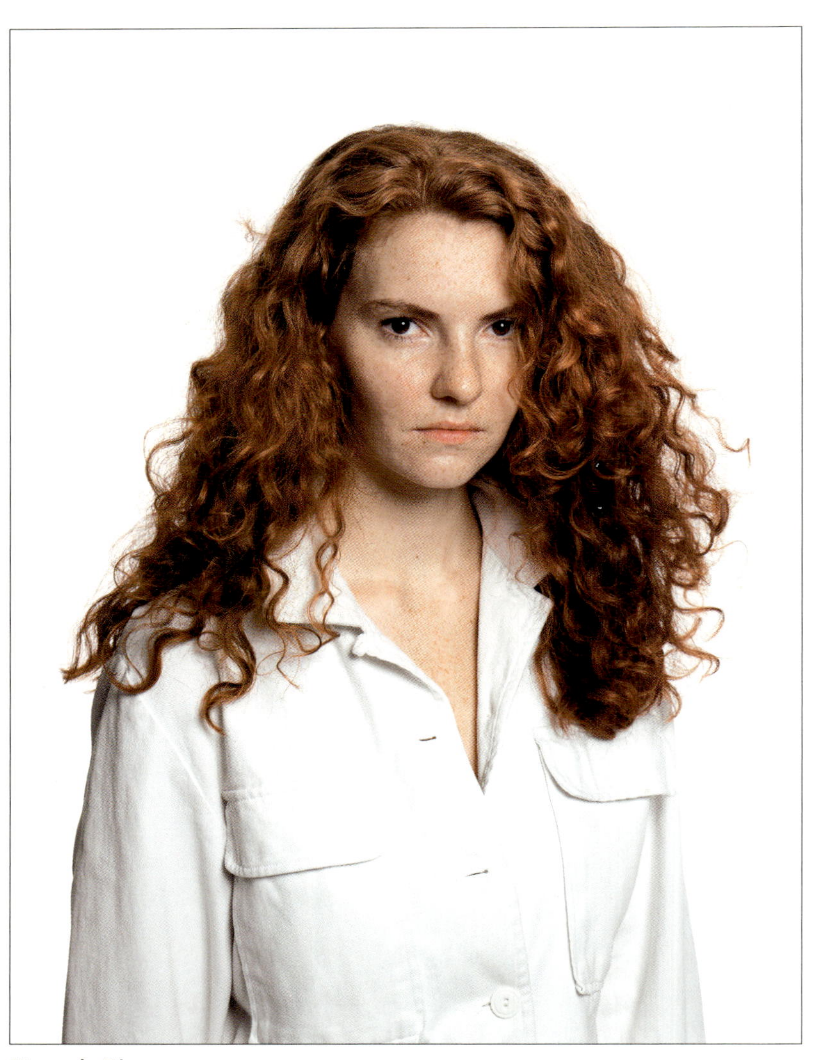

Manuela Diemer

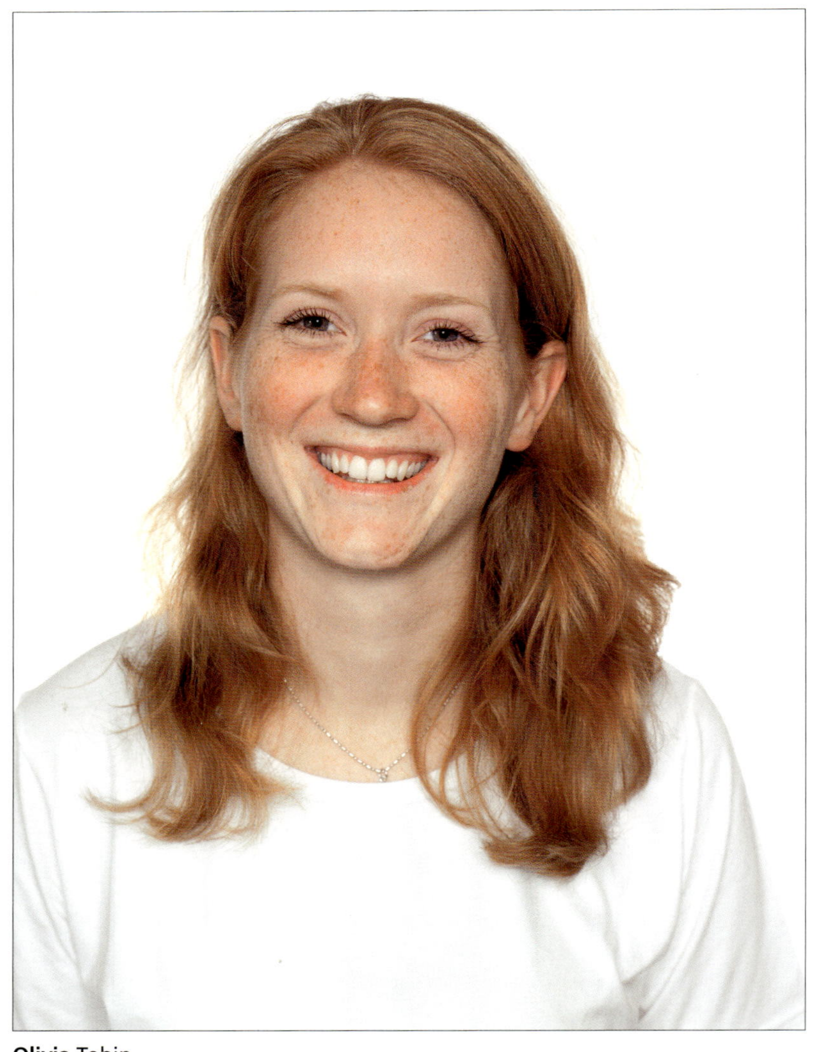

Olivia Tobin

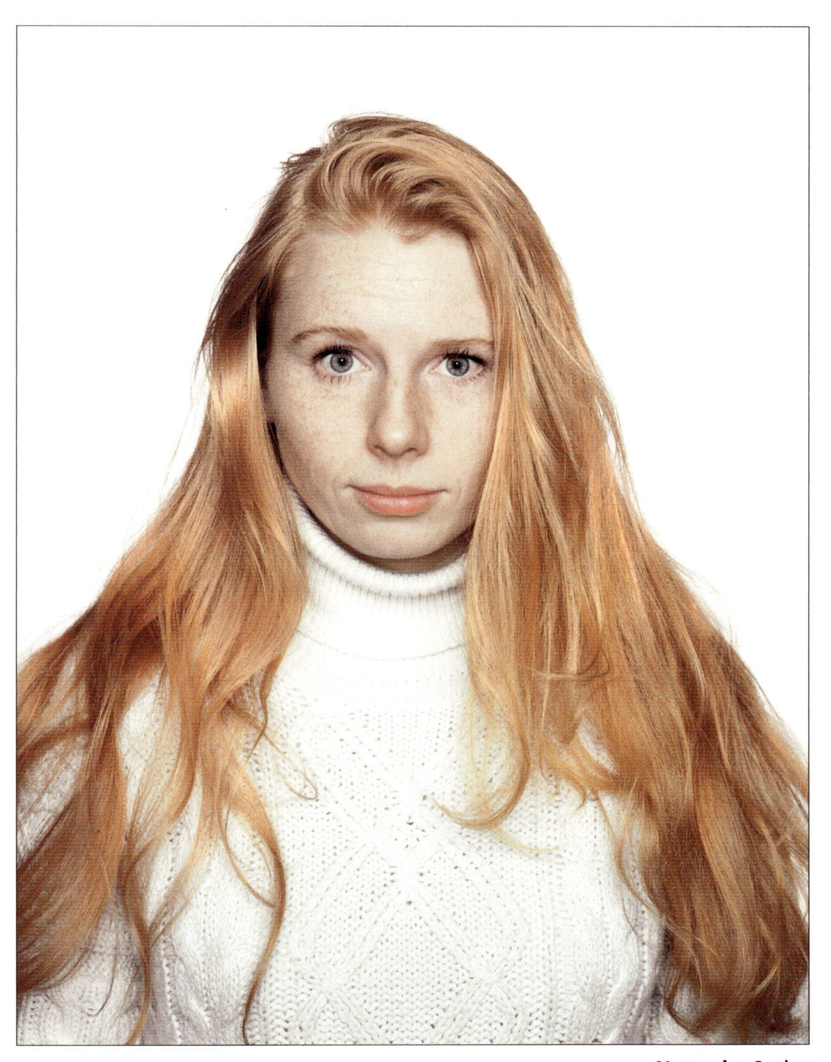

Natascha Satler

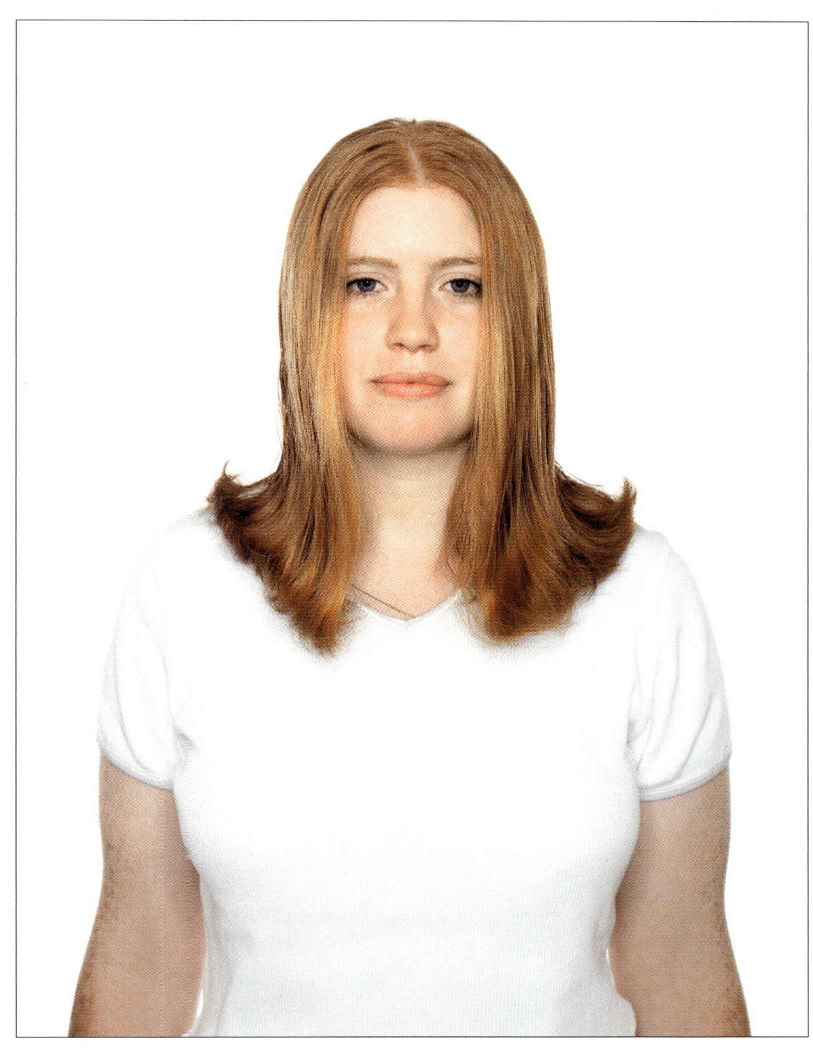

Adrienne O'Dwyer

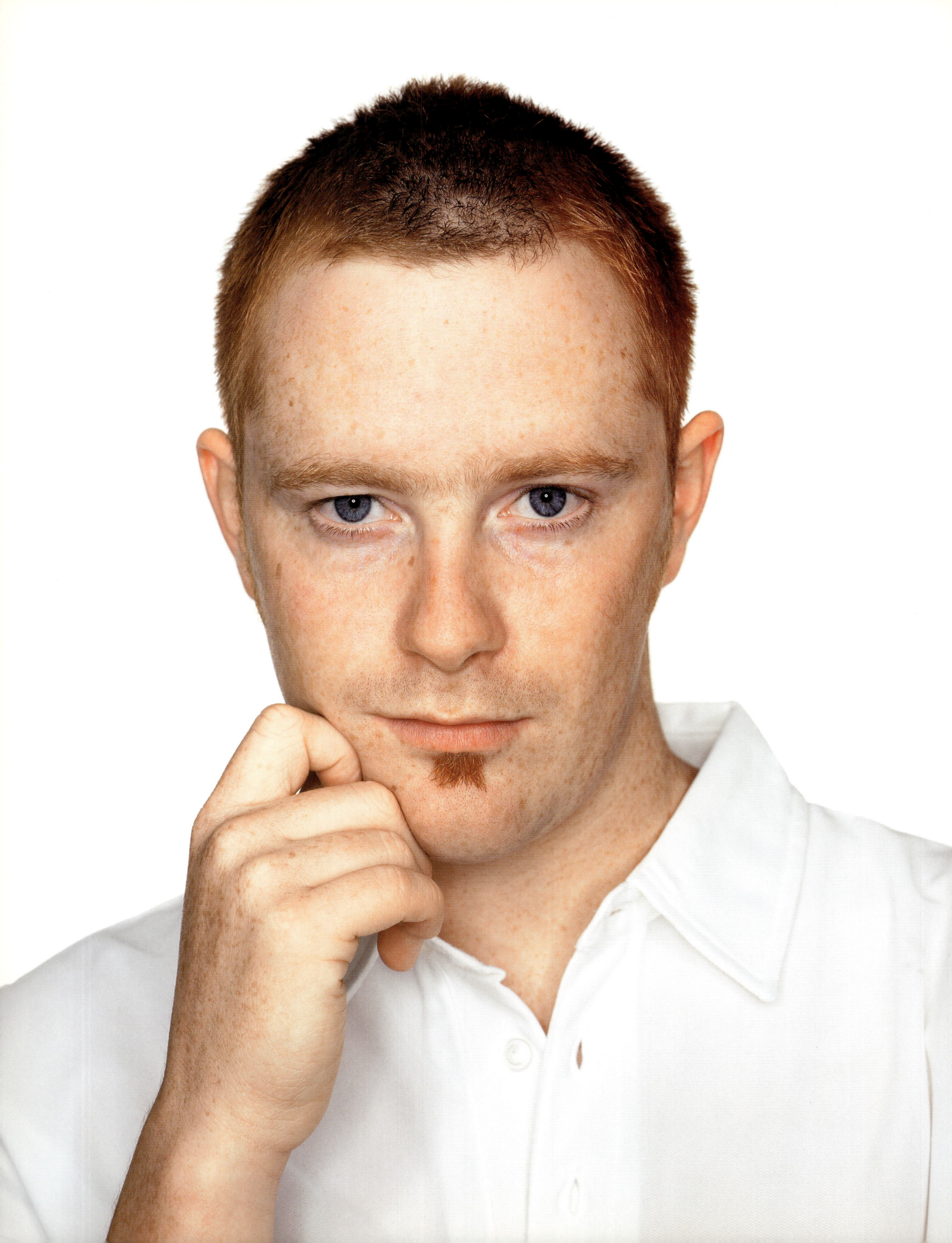

"Nobody messes with a redhead!"

"Fire and Gasoline!"

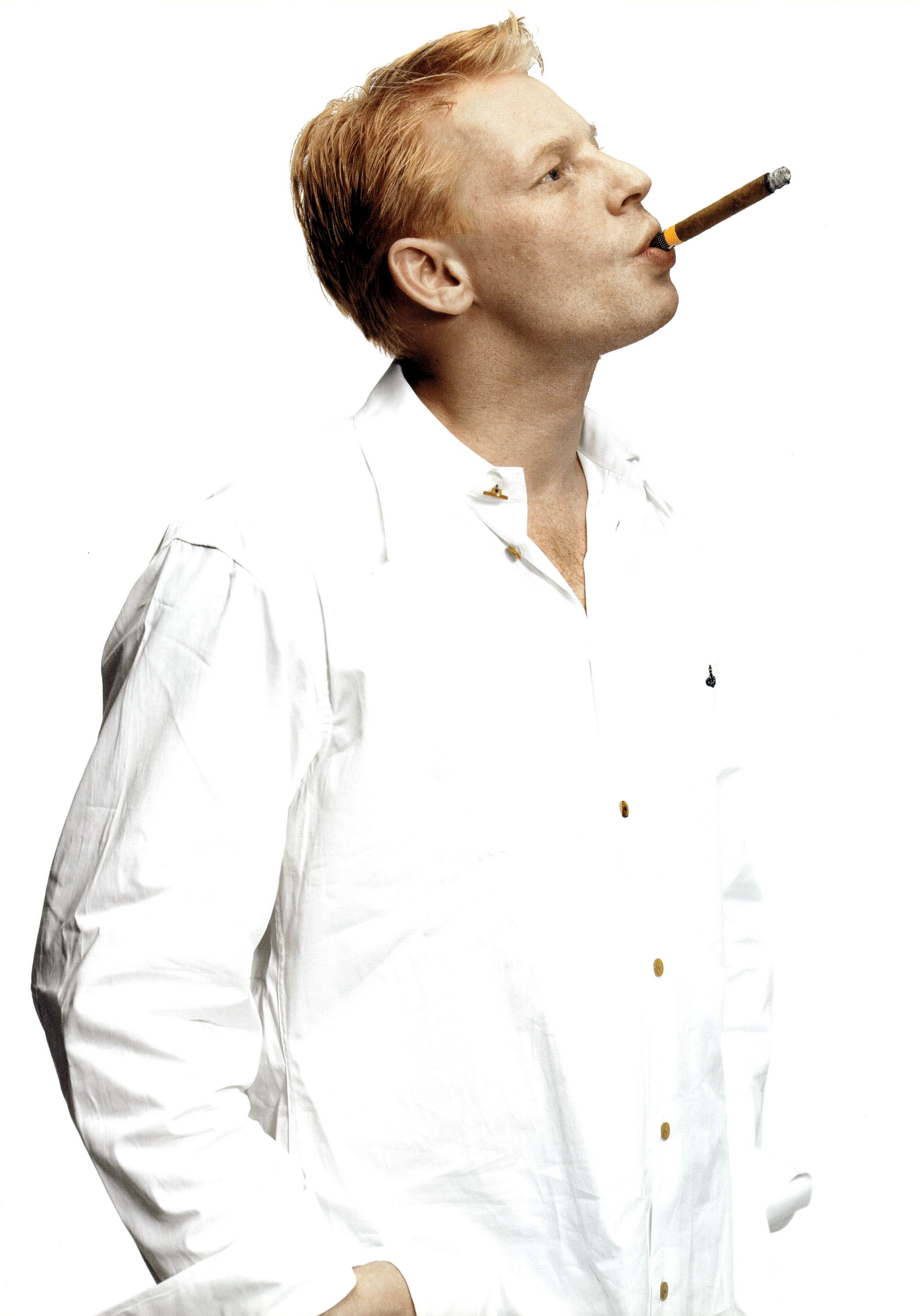

"A young woman once said to me
she would never get involved with somebody
with red hair,
even if he was a great guy."

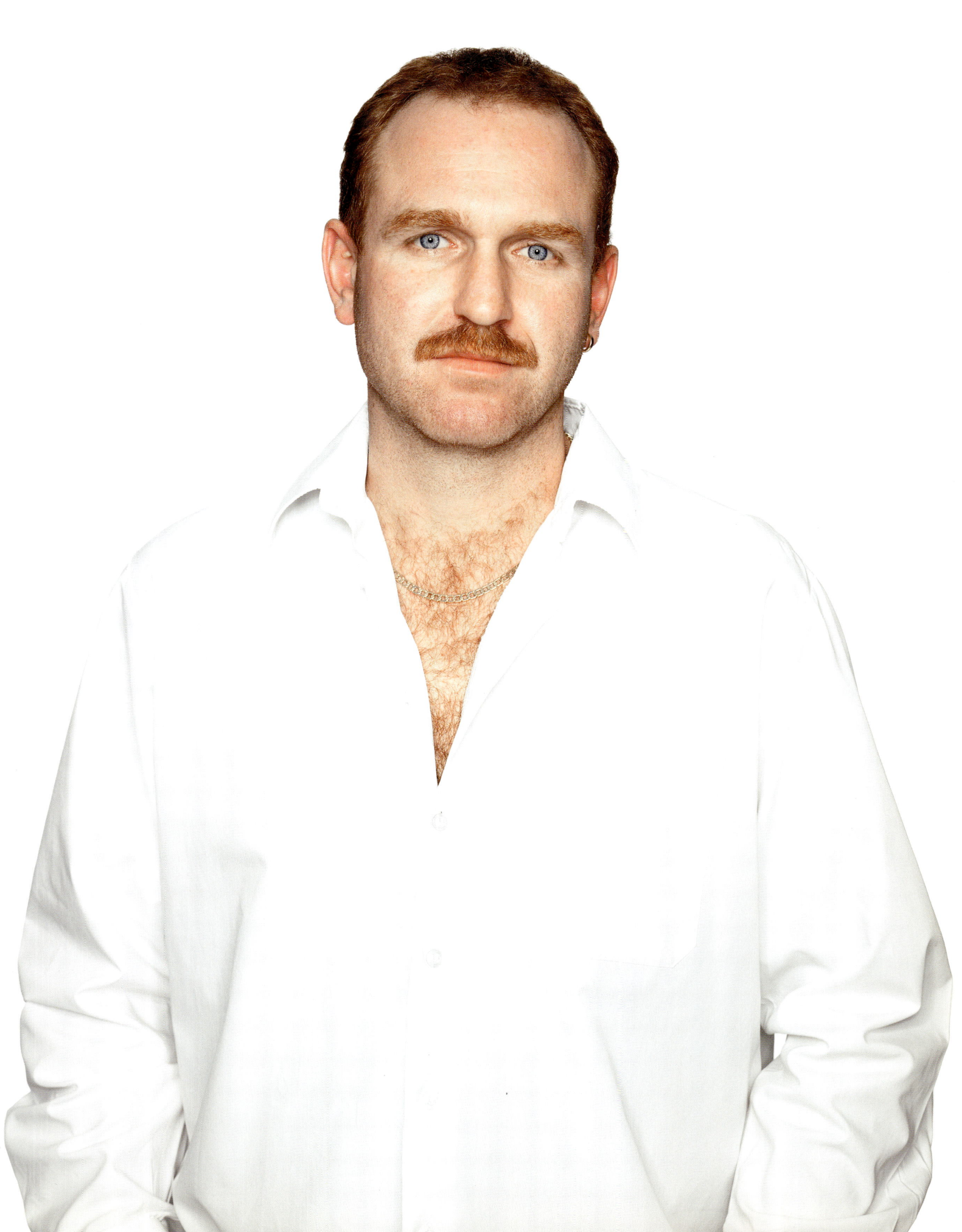

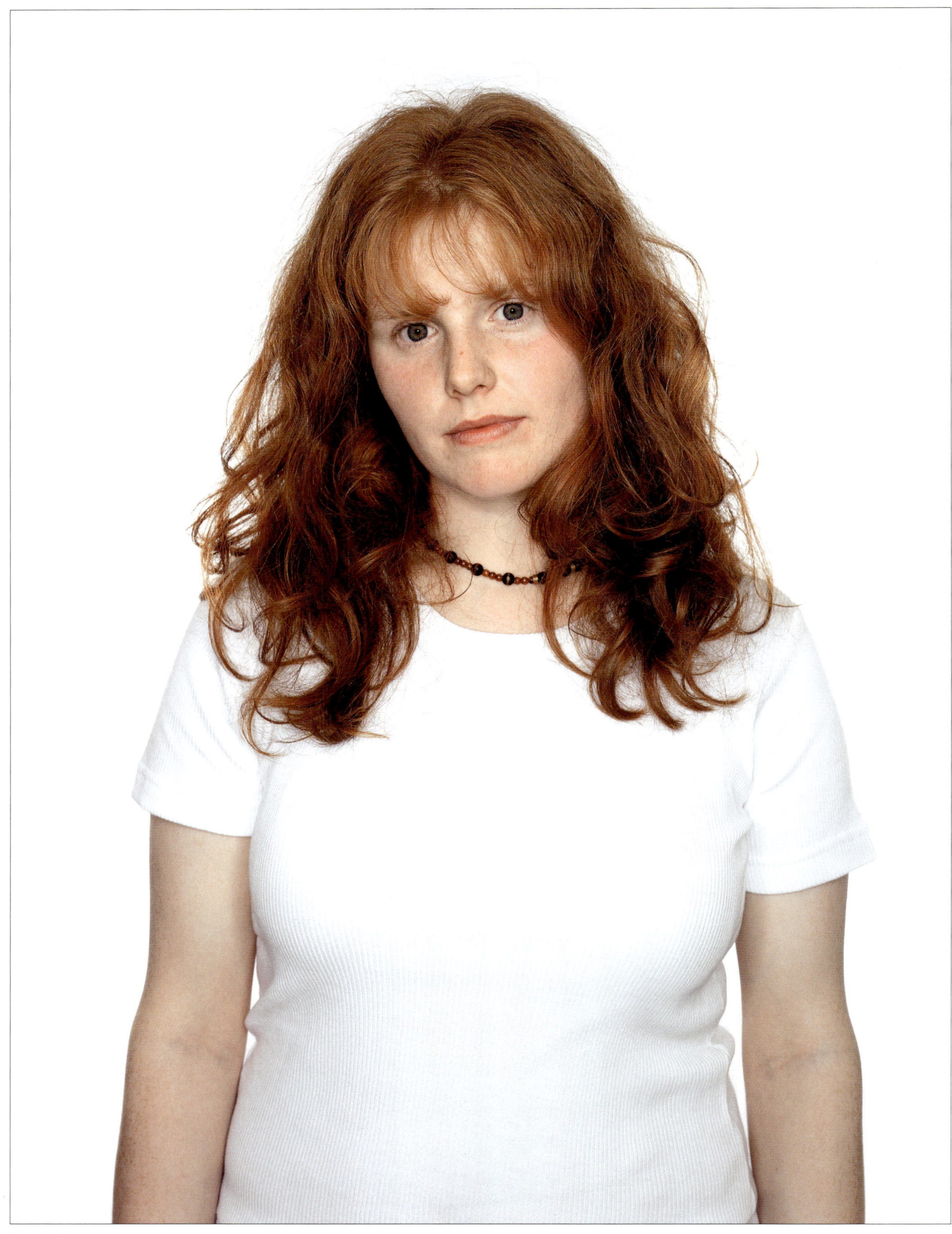

Karen Brennan

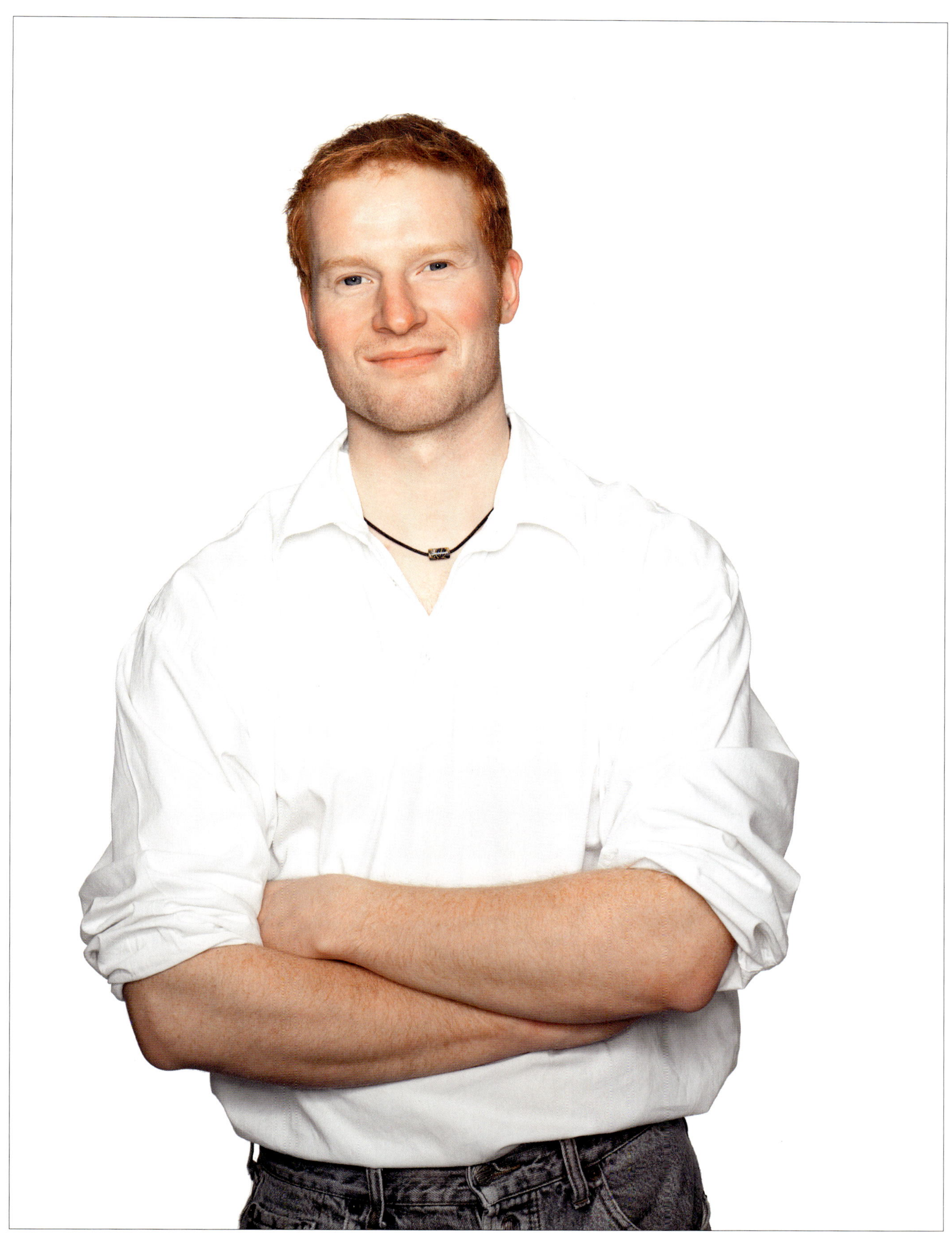

Alexander Kapp

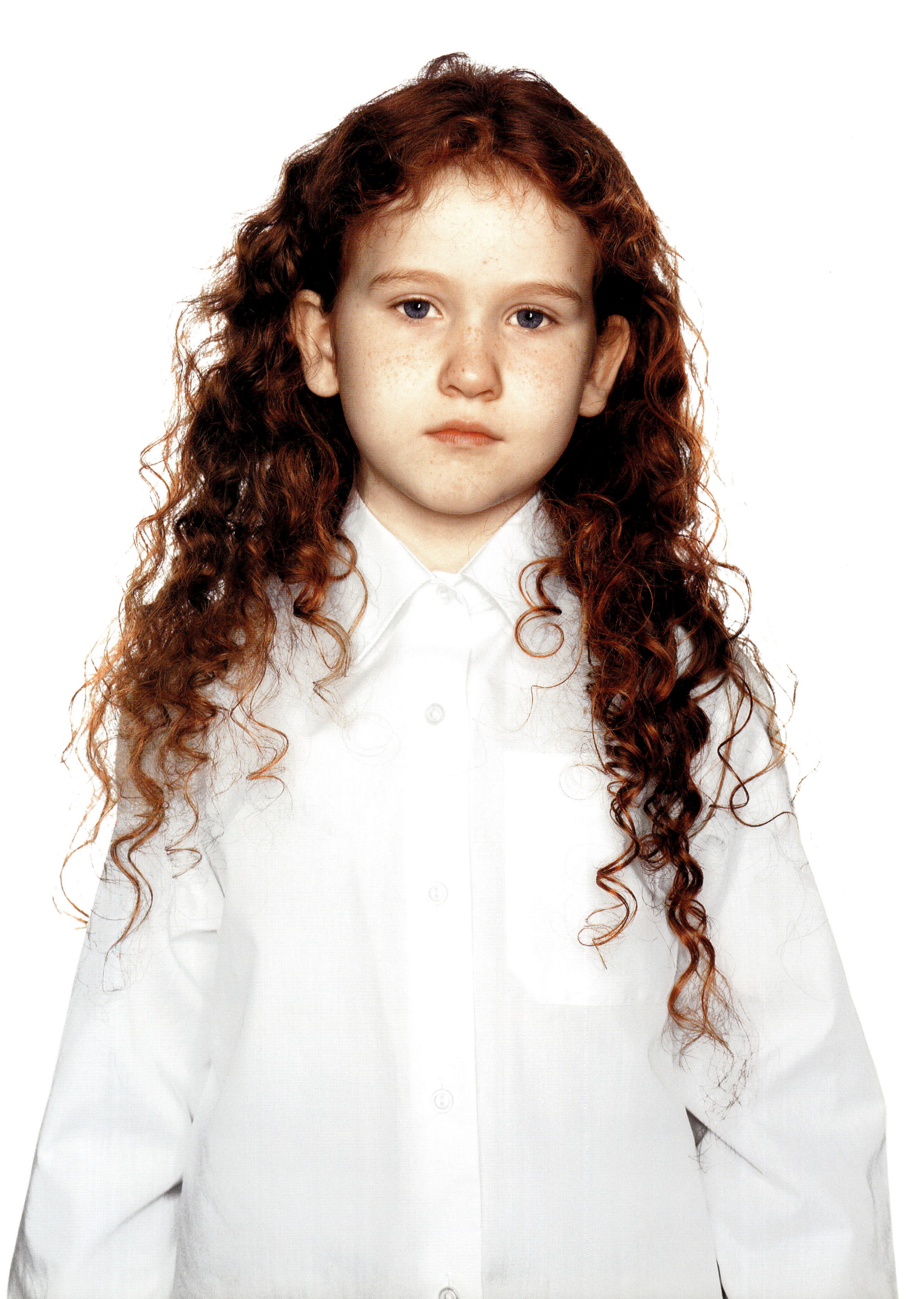

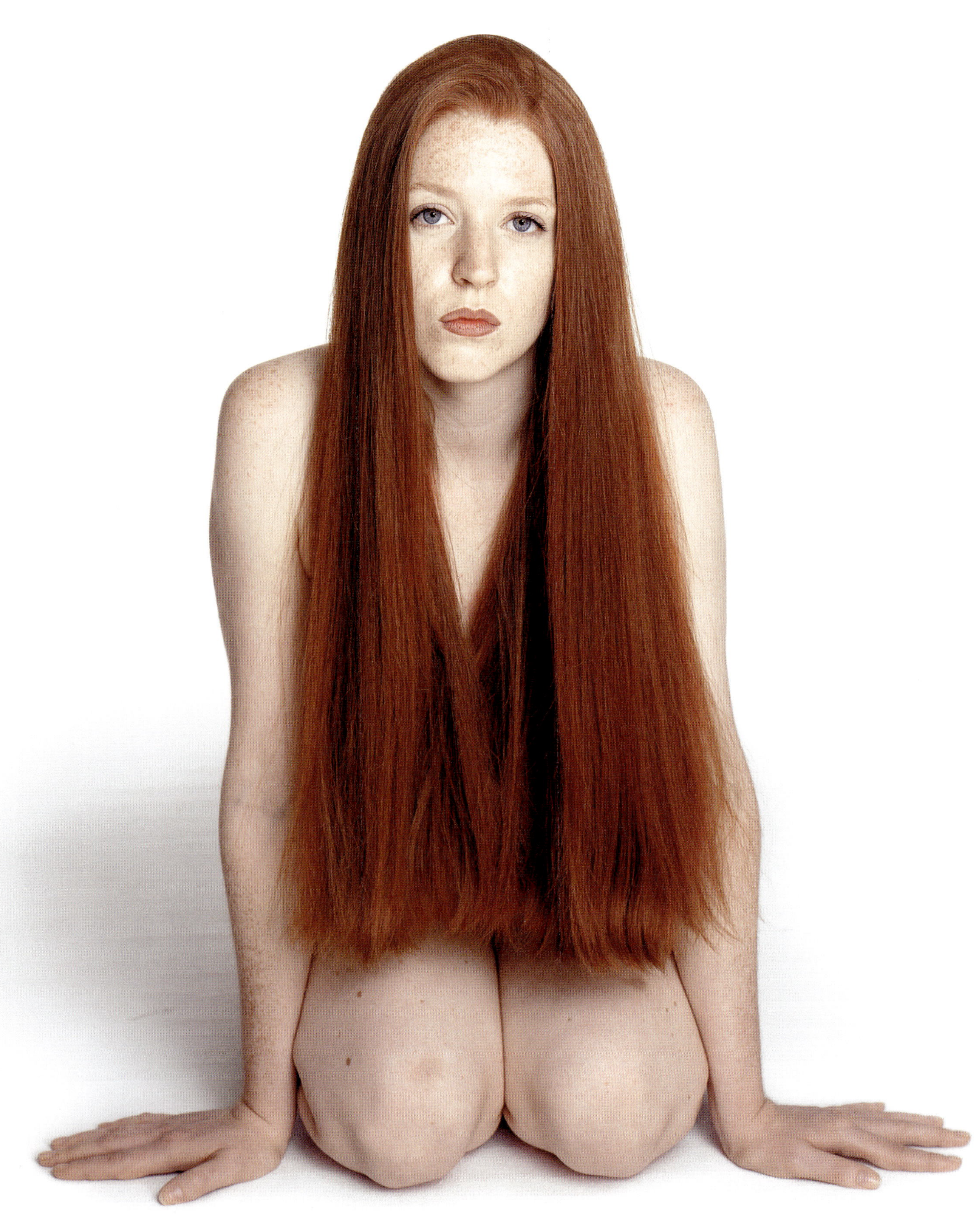

I am what I am

Uwe Ditz

Our hair gives a certain feeling for life, although our feelings may often be contradictory. When I was small, people always said: "You've got red hair." I simply didn't understand what they were talking about. I always felt there was something artificial about the color red. The fire truck in my picture book was red. The little red figure in the pedestrian signals, too. But my hair?

The grown-ups often said: "That little guy sure has nice hair." Of course, that's the sort of thing anybody would like to hear. On the other hand, there were the things that happened in primary school. Like when the whole class taunted me, "Carrot top, carrot top." I can still remember the way the teacher suddenly turned up and demanded: "Who said that?" Two boys had to go up to the front of the classroom and apologize to me in front of everyone. That was the end of that for the time being. At least on the surface of things. But something stuck in my mind after these experiences: you're different from the others.

Redheads are a minority. Only one percent of all people living in Germany has red hair. Think about it: one hundred people gathered together on a square, and only one of them is like you. That really is a weird feeling. I believe that our looks shape us from our childhood onwards. This effect is often stronger than we would like to admit. When I was around twelve, this was one of the main issues of my life: those wiry, red curls that never did want I wanted. And the fair complexion. This probably annoyed me even more. I've got no idea how often I had a sunburn. When we went to the swimming pool, the others always got a tan. But I just turned red as a lobster, then my skin peeled off and I was white again. Just great!

Beauty is a flexible word. But when you're going through puberty it means not being different from the others. You want to belong and search for your identity by conforming to a certain set of rules. Girls with long hair are good-looking. So are guys with short hair: blonde, brown or black. But what about red? When the guy sitting next to me at school with the smooth, blonde hair got love letters and I didn't, I was certainly tempted to blame my hair.

When I was sixteen, I first began to really deal with my hair. I think that, at this age, many people observe their outward appearance and their inner self with a certain degree of objectivity. And both—the outer and the inner self—are intrinsically linked. Was I perhaps something special? Anyway, my self-confidence began to grow, perhaps partly due to my discovery that many women are strongly attracted to redheads. They were the ones who were particularly envious of my hair. But then I also began to hear more and more compliments: "Red hair is great. Something special. Be glad." And I was. I grew my hair long, down past my shoulders. I was proud of every red centimeter of it.

Today, I can certainly say that my red hair has played an important role in my search for my own identity. At least subconsciously. I hated it, was in awe of it, felt unnerved by it. And then—I began to like it. Blonde hair? Smooth hair? No thanks! I am what I am.

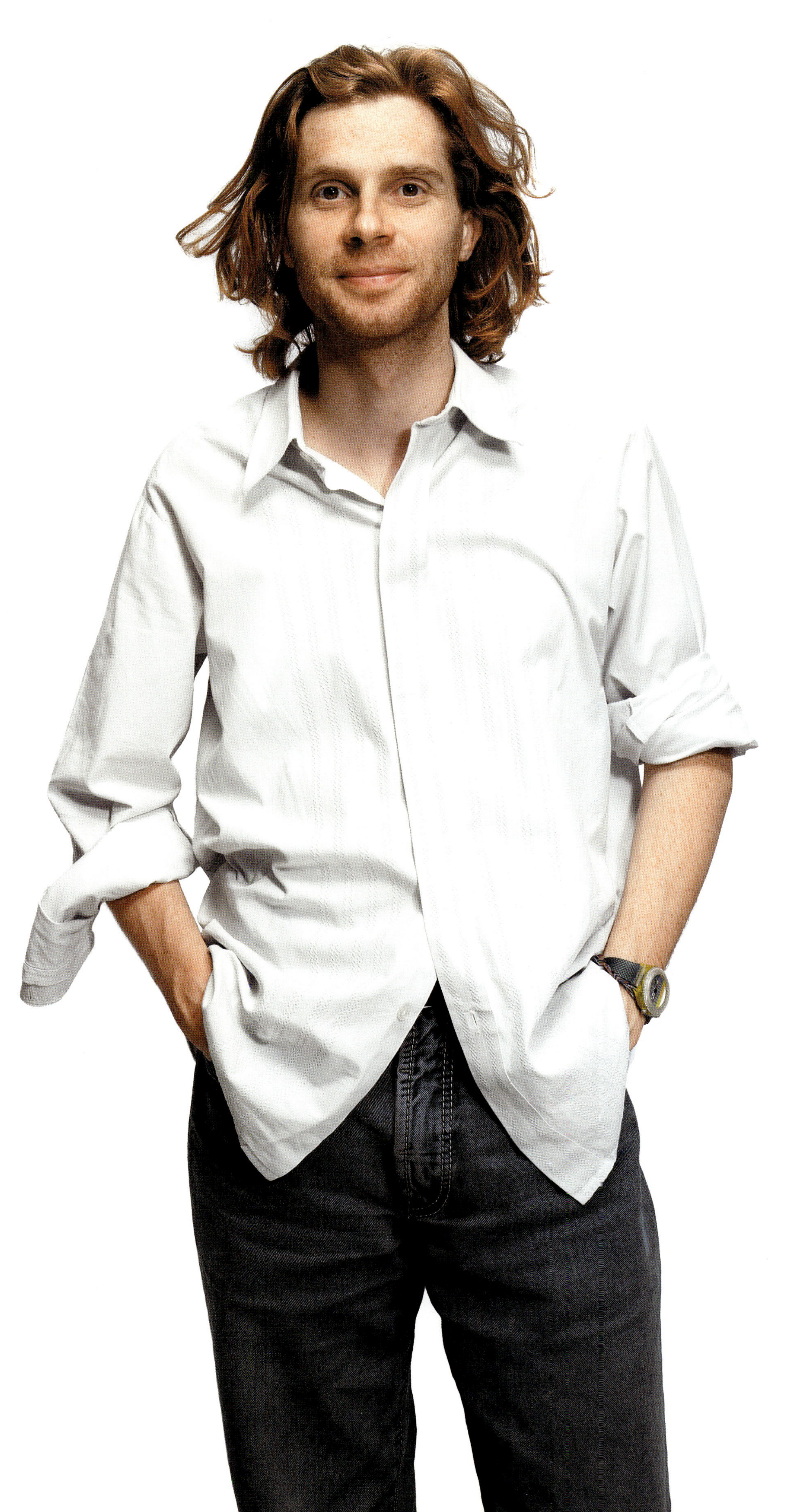

Uwe Ditz

Uwe Ditz was born in Stuttgart, Germany, in 1963. After finishing his O-levels at school he went on to complete training as a photolaboratory technician. He then worked for two years as a photographer at the Institute for Scientific Photography and Cinematography at M. P. Kage, Schloß Weißenstein (Germany). Ditz turned to commercial photography so as to work more closely with other people. He concentrated for two years on the areas "Still-life" and "People." Following this he completed his A-levels at the Vocational College for Design in Schwäbisch Gmünd. After three years of working as a photographer's assistant for German and English photographers both at home and abroad (e.g. in London, France and the USA), Uwe Ditz became freelance, focusing on people, portrait, fashion and still-life photography.

Uwe Ditz has been able to develop his own style as a photographer through a variety of different projects such as advertising campaigns for jeans, a milieu study consisting of 260 portraits of workers, and a photographic chronicle of all exhibits at the Titanic Exhibition in Hamburg. In addition, he won the 1994 Kodak-Sponsor-Prize for color portraits.

Barry Egan

Barry Egan, born in 1967 in Dublin, is the Culture Editor of *The Sunday Independent*, Ireland's biggest national newspaper. He did his first interview when he was 17 with Morrissey of *The Smiths.* Since then he has interviewed Bono, the *Rolling Stones, Guns 'n Roses,* Sinead O'Connor, Cher, supermodel Eva Herzigova, Juliette Binoche, Patsy Kensit, fashion designer Vivien Westwood, the Italian porn MP Cicciolina and most recently the Irish Prime Minister Bertie Ahern. He covered the U2 "Zoo TV" tour in the early Nineties, following the band around the world. Reprinted in *Creem Magazine* in America, *Rock* in Italy and *The Express* in England, Egan's highly critical views on U2 in *The Sunday Independent* did not go down well with band or their management. Barry Egan was in Rwanda in 1994 to witness the devastating aftermath of the genocide there. He was also in Albania to write about the plight for the Kosovar refugees during the war in Kosovo in April 1999. He plans to go back later this year.

Irmela Hannover

Irmela Hannover was born in Bremen, Germany, in 1954. She is the eldest of four red-headed sisters, a blonde brother and a brunette sister. After gaining an additional qualification by studying jurisprudence at the German Institute for Third World Policy, she worked for two years in Brazil as part of a UN development aid program. In 1985 she returned to Cologne and worked for West German Radio as a trainee. In 1987 she became part of the editorial staff and later hosted the ARD-Legal Advice show. She now also works as chief editor for the WDR parent's program *Kind und Kegel.* Irmela Hannover is the mother of three non-redheaded children and author of *Frauen mit roten Haaren (Women with Red Hair),* which was published in 1997 by Rütten & Lönig.

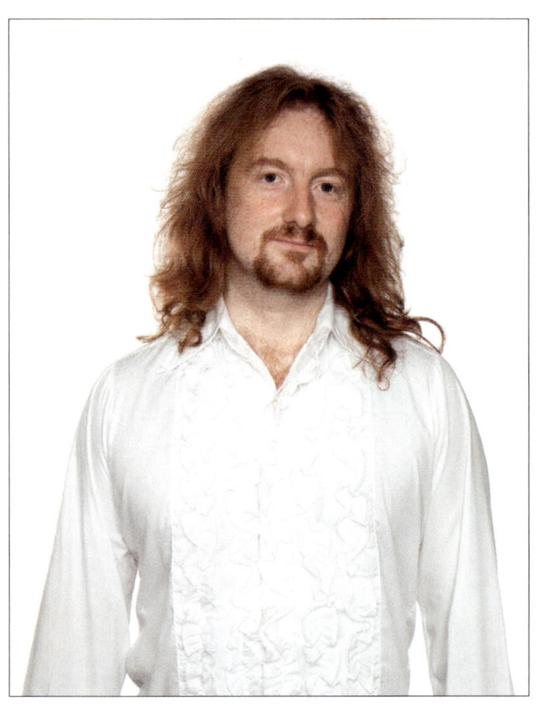

Barry Egan

Irmela Hannover

I would especially like to thank my wife Susanne and my parents.

Special thanks are also due to my assistants Dominik Westermann, Stephanie Müller and Kerstin Härtel and to my trainees Tanja Hegedüß and Diana Lauer.

I would also like to thank Elena & Markus Krämer, Johannes Zimmermann, Christoph Just (Jot + Jot), Elisabeth Husendörfer, Kerstin Wacker & Henrik Hitzebleck and Ivica Kolaric.

In addition, I am very grateful to Diaservice, Stuttgart, Harvey's Guest House, Dublin, and recom GmbH, Ostfildern, for their support.

Translation from the German by Julian Cooper
Editorial direction by Sara Schindler
Layout by Giorgio Chiappa
Lithography and Imaging by Marion Zeh, recom GmbH, Ostfildern, Germany
Printed by Spefa Druck AG, Zurich, Switzerland
Bound by Eibert AG, Eschenbach, Switzerland

ISBN 3-908163-17-X